Phyllis Schlafly Speaks, Volume 5

Stopping the ERA

Phyllis Schlafly

Edited by Ed Martin

Permission to quote in critical reviews with citation:
Stopping the ERA
By Phyllis Schlafly

ISBN 978-1-949718-01-0

Skellig
AMERICA

TABLE OF CONTENTS

Dedication
Introduction by Ed Martin   i
A Short History of ERA   1
What's Wrong With "Equal Rights" for Women   17
The Fraud Called the Equal Rights Amendment   33
Dear State Legislator: The Buck Stops With You   45
ERA Won't Help Women in Education   60
How ERA Will Hurt Divorced Women   64
How ERA Will Affect Social Security   72
ERA Means Abortion & Population Shrinkage   76
ERA Will Doom Fraternities & Sororities   89
How ERA Will Affect Churches & Private Schools   97
How ERA Will Affect Athletics   106
The Hypocrisy of ERA Proponents   113
Who Will Profit from ERA?   126
ERA & Women's Colleges   129
What Really Happened in Houston   133
How ERA Will Raise Insurance Rates   147
Ruth Bader Ginsburg's Feminist World View   150
About Phyllis Schlafly & Ed Martin   165

To all the men and women who accepted
her call to be Phyllis Schlafly Eagles:
You stopped the ERA, kept America pro-life,
and helped Make America Great Again.
Today, your work looms bigger than ever
and your love for America is the heart of our nation.

and

To Sister Maria Battista of the Lamb of God, O.C.D.:

Thank you for your witness to a life of prayer and service
to the Lord that echoes grandmother's daily prayer and service
to God. Phyllis was so proud of you. Please pray for us.

Introduction by Ed Martin

L ate in 1971, the U.S. House of Representatives approved the Equal Rights Amendment (ERA) by a vote of 354 to 23. A few months later in early 1972, ERA was passed by the U.S. Senate 84 to 8. As part of the deal to pass ERA, an expiration deadline was put on this amendment: March 22, 1979. The ERA was sent to the states for ratification. Within a year, half of the states had voted to ratify ERA.

But something happened over the next 7 years—or better *someone* happened. One woman stepped forward and led a movement opposing ERA: Phyllis Schlafly. By its expiration date in 1979, the ERA had been passed by 36 states, but 5 states had changed their position and voted to *rescind* ratification. In response to the failure, President Jimmy Carter and Congress scrambled to extend the expiration deadline—they succeeded in adding 3 more years—but it was not enough to stop Phyllis and her band of STOP ERA sisters. By the time this new deadline arrived—June 30, 1982—ERA still had failed to pass enough states. It was dead.

What could *possibly* be wrong with an Equal Rights Amendment? After all, everybody believes in equal rights, right? And this belief is *especially even essentially* American: our great founding Independence was, after all, through God's gift to each of us equally—the rights to life, liberty and the pursuit of happiness.

In the early 1970s, coming on the heels of the Civil Rights Movement, equal rights sounded so good. But the devil was in the details of the ERA. The ERA was an effort to INSERT sex into the Constitution (nowhere does the document refer to man or woman— only citizen!) and the impact would be massive. It would mandate abortion paid for by tax dollars. It would require women in combat. It would strip meaning form sex designation—eliminating single sex schools and forcing men into women's bathrooms and vice versa.

The battle over ERA was a political David v. Goliath.

For ERA: three Presidents, President Nixon, Ford, and Carter and their wives along with Lady Bird Johnson; Nearly all of Congress and governors from over 40 states; the media—from Walter Cronkite to Phil Donahue and every major print and media outlet; and especially the loud feminists—from Ruth Bader Ginsburg to Bella Abzug to Betty Friedan.

But there was more: far too many who called themselves conservatives—including Bill Buckley and his National Review— stood down from the fight to stop the Equal Rights Amendment.

The opposition to ERA was led by the "Lady from Alton," Phyllis Schlafly and her band of wives and mothers. Her grassroots were well-trained as Phyllis drew from her over 30 years in politics. What was unique—historic!—was Phyllis' ability to build an opposition: in message and army. Her army became the testing ground from the later incarnations of the Moral Majority and Christian Coalition: unity of purpose over an issue and politics AND disregard of differences to pursue an end. In the case of ERA for example, Phyllis was the first to unite Protestants, Catholics, Mormons and Jews into a historic faith-based movement.

This book includes some reference to how Phyllis formed her army and maintained it. But it is more about her message. In crystal clear language, Phyllis laid out the reasons to oppose ERA and how to argue the opposition. Her Phyllis Schlafly Report from February 1972 might be the most powerful pamphlet since Thomas Paine—it was passed along from state house to state house and described as "what beat ERA" more than once.

But her messaging skills did not stop at writing. She taught her team how to lead in public. Her own role especially in earned media was accelerated by the scores of appearances on The Phil Donahue Show and culminating with the famous Meet The Press appearance from Houston in 1977. While the government sponsored National Women's Conference met across town led by Bella Abzug and others, Phyllis pulled tens of thousands of people to her own conference. The images of pro-abortion radicals at Abzug's event contrasted with Phyllis' regular American women rocketed across the media and nation and are often cited as turning the tide in the fight.

One last point on message: Phyllis—through trial and error—honed in on messages that worked particularly well for that moment in American life. For example, in the years after the Vietnam War, few Americans had support for women combat and the ERA would force the drafting of our daughters into battle. This moved mothers and fathers to oppose ERA.

What is often missed about the STOP ERA effort is the scope of the genius of Phyllis Schlafly. In one movement over one decade, Phyllis revolutionized at least three political tactics: grassroots organization, direct communication, and inter-faith leadership.

In fact, and much to the chagrin of the feminists, Phyllis was the greatest American woman. She used to say she "had it all—just not all at once" and she meant it. She worked her way through college testing ammunition during World War II. With a graduate degree from Harvard, she was an early employee of the American Enterprise Institute in D.C. quickly returned to her hometown of St. Louis to manage a successful campaign for Congress at 24 years old.

A few years later, she was a married housewife in Alton, Illinois. She started her big family—six children—and settled into a not-so-quiet life. By her early 40s, she was a world-renowned expert on the threat of Soviet Communism and writing books with leading military leaders on the "strategic balance" and the need for a Space missile defense program. She launched the conservative movement with *A Choice Not An Echo* which eventually yielded President Ronald Reagan.

After she beat ERA, Phyllis "settled" into the life as a leading conservative. She beat the pro-abortion Republicans who tried to drop her pro-life plank from the platform. And she saw, long before anyone else, the true genius—and conservatism—of Donald J. Trump. That she died a few weeks before Trump's election (Mr. Trump attended Phyllis' funeral), didn't matter—she saw it from her perch on high.

This is the fifth volume of Phyllis Schlafly Speaks, the collection of Phyllis Schlafly's writings. It is not exhaustive on her writings on ERA but representative. For more, please contact the Phyllis Schlafly Archives at the Eagle Forum Education and Legal Defense Fund - www.PhyllisSchlafly.com and (314) 721-1213.

Chapter 1
A Short History of ERA
September 1986

T he Equal Rights Amendment (ERA), a proposed amendment to the United States Constitution, was born in the era of the women's suffrage amendment and first introduced into Congress in 1923. For nearly 50 years, all those Congresses had the good judgment to leave ERA buried in Committee. Almost no one of importance or prominence in either political party supported it.

During most of those years, ERA had attached to it the Hayden Clause which read: "Nothing in this Amendment will be construed to deprive persons of the female sex of any of the rights, benefits, and exemptions now conferred by law on persons of the female sex." Then, as now, the advocates were unwilling to compromise for anything less than a doctrinaire equality, and so ERA went nowhere.

In 1971, when feminism first rushed onto the scene in the United States, a little band of women stormed the corridors of Congress and demanded the discharge from committee of the long-dormant ERA. The House passed ERA on October 12, 1971, after rejecting the Wiggins Amendment which would have exempted women from "compulsory military service" and which also would have preserved other laws "which reasonably promote the health and safety of the people." Only 23 Congressmen voted no, of whom one was the senior female member, Representative Leonor Sullivan (D-MO), who made a strong speech opposing ERA because it would harm the family.

In the Senate, Senator Sam J. Ervin, Jr., (D-NC) proposed nine separate amendments to ERA to protect the traditional rights of women. Every one was defeated on a roll-call vote on March 21 and 22, 1972. These nine amendments established the legislative history that ERA was intended to do exactly what the Ervin Amendments would have prevented ERA from doing.

The Ervin amendments would have exempted women from compulsory military service and from combat duty; they would have protected the traditional rights of wives, mothers and widows, and preserved the responsibility of fathers to support their children; they would have preserved laws that secure privacy to males and females; they would have continued the laws that make sexual offenses punishable as crimes. All these modifying clauses were defeated. When ERA was passed in strict, absolute language, only nine Senators voted "no."

Congress sent ERA out to the states on March 22,1972. Within twelve months, 30 states had ratified ERA. Then the disillusionment set in. In the next six years, only five more states ratified ERA, but five of the 30 states rescinded their previous ratifications of ERA, leaving a net score of zero for six years of lobbying for ERA. The five states that rescinded their previous ratifications were Nebraska, Tennessee, Idaho, Kentucky, and South

Dakota. The following 15 states never ratified ERA: Alabama, Arizona, Arkansas, Florida, Georgia, Illinois, Louisiana, Mississippi, Missouri, Nevada, North Carolina, Oklahoma, South Carolina, Utah, and Virginia.

Most of the 15 states which never ratified ERA were forced by the ERA advocates to vote on ERA again and again. The Illinois Legislature voted on ERA every year from 1972 through 1982, the Florida Legislature nearly every year, the North Carolina and Oklahoma Legislatures every two years. Most of these votes were highly controversial, intensely debated, with much media coverage and many spectators present.

During the ratification period, ERA was enthusiastically supported by 99 percent of the media, the Gerald Ford and Jimmy Carter Administrations, most public officials at every level of government, and many wealthy national organizations. ERA enjoyed the political momentum of what appeared to be inevitable victory.

A small group of women in 1972, under the name "Stop ERA," took on what seemed to be an impossible task. In 1975, they founded "Eagle Forum"—the genesis of the pro-family movement, a coming together of believers of all faiths who, for the first time, worked together toward a shared political goal. Eagle Forum volunteers persevered through the years and led the movement to final victory over ERA.

The last state to ratify ERA was Indiana in January 1977. There have been perhaps 25 different votes on ERA since that time (in legislatures, committees, referenda, and Congress), but Indiana was ERA's last success.

The Debates About ERA

The Equal Rights Amendment was presented to the American public as something that would benefit women, "put women in the U.S. Constitution," and lift women out of their so-called "second-class citizenship." However, in thousands of debates, the ERA advocates were unable to show any way that ERA would benefit women or end any discrimination against them. The fact is that women already enjoy every constitutional right that men enjoy and have enjoyed equal employment opportunity since 1964.

In the short term, clever advertising and packaging can sell a worthless product. But, in the long term, the American people cannot be fooled. ERA'S biggest defect was that it had nothing to offer American women.

The opponents of ERA, on the other hand, were able to show many harms that ERA would cause.

1. ERA would take away legal rights that women possessed—not confer any new rights on women.

a) ERA would take away women's traditional exemption from military conscription and also from military combat duty. The classic "sex discriminatory" laws are those which say that "male citizens of age 18" must register for the draft and those which exempt women from military combat assignment. The ERAers tried to get around this argument by asking the Supreme Court to hold that the 14th Amendment already requires women to be drafted, but they lost in 1981 in Rostker v. Goldberg when the Supreme Court upheld

4

the traditional exemption of women from the draft under our present Constitution.

b) ERA would take away the traditional benefits in the law for wives, widows and mothers. ERA would make unconstitutional the laws, which then existed in every state, that impose on a husband the obligation to support his wife.

2. ERA would take away important rights and powers of the states and confer these on other branches of government which are farther removed from the people.

a) ERA would give enormous power to the Federal courts to decide the definitions of the words in ERA, "sex" and "equality of rights." It is irresponsible to leave it to the courts to decide such sensitive, emotional and important issues as whether or not the language applies to abortion or homosexual rights.

b) Section II of ERA would give enormous new powers to the Federal Government that now belong to the states. ERA would give Congress the power to legislate on all those areas of law which include traditional differences of treatment on account of sex: marriage, property laws, divorce and alimony, child custody, adoptions, abortion, homosexual laws, sex crimes, private and public schools, prison regulations, and insurance. ERA would thus result in the massive redistribution of powers in our Federal system.

3. ERA's impact on education would take away rights from women students, upset many customs and practices, and bring government intrusion into private schools.

a) ERA would force all schools and colleges, and all the programs and athletics they conduct, to be fully coeducational and sex-integrated. ERA would make unconstitutional all the current exceptions in Title IX which allow for single-sex schools and colleges and for separate treatment of the sexes for certain activities. ERA would mean the end of single-sex colleges. ERA would force the sex integration of fraternities, sororities, Boy Scouts, Girl Scouts, YMCA, YWCA, Boys State and Girls State conducted by the American Legion, and mother-daughter and father-son school events.

b) ERA would risk the income tax exemption of all private schools and colleges that make any difference of treatment between males and females, even though no public monies are involved. ERA is a statement of public policy that would apply the same rules to sex that we now observe on race, and it is clear that no school that makes any racial distinctions may enjoy tax exemption.

4. ERA would put abortion rights into the U.S. Constitution, and make abortion funding a new constitutional right. Roe v. Wade in 1973 legalized abortion, but the fight to make abortion funding a constitutional right was lost in Harris v. McRae in 1980. The abortionists then looked to ERA to force taxpayer funding. The American Civil Liberties Union filed briefs in abortion cases in Hawaii, Massachusetts, Pennsylvania and Connecticut arguing that, since abortion is a medical procedure performed only on women, it is "sex discrimination" within the meaning of the state's ERA to deny tax funding for abortions. In the most recent decision, the Connecticut Superior Court ruled on April 19,1986 that the state ERA requires abortion funding. Those who oppose tax funding of abortions demand that ERA be amended to prevent this effect, but

ERA advocates want ERA only so long as it includes abortion funding.

5. ERA would put "gay rights" into the U.S. Constitution, because the word in the Amendment is "sex" not women. Eminent authorities have stated that ERA would legalize the granting of marriage licenses to homosexuals and generally implement the "gay rights" and lesbian agenda. These authorities include the Yale Law Journal, the leading textbook on sex discrimination used in U.S. law schools, Harvard Law Professor Paul Freund, and Senator Sam J. Ervin, Jr. Other lawyers have disputed this effect, but no one can guarantee that the courts would not define the word "sex" to include "preference" just as they have defined "sex" to include pregnancy.

6. In the final years of the ERA battle, two new arguments appeared. Both were advanced by the ERA advocates, but they quickly became arguments in the hands of the ERA opponents.

a) ERA would require "unisex insurance," that is, would prohibit insurance companies from charging lower rates for women, even though actuarial data clearly show that women, as a group, are entitled to lower rates both for automobile accident insurance and life insurance. This is because women drivers have fewer accidents and women live longer than men. Most people found it a peculiar argument that "women's rights" should include the "right" to pay higher insurance rates.

b) ERA would eliminate veterans' preference. This rests on the same type of legal argument as the abortion funding argument: since most veterans are men, it is claimed that it is "sex discriminatory" to give them benefits. Naturally, this argument was not acceptable to the veterans, and their national organizations lobbied hard against ERA.

The Houston Debacle

Realizing that the seven-year time period allowed for ratification was running out, the ERA advocates in 1977 persuaded Congress to give them $5 million, supposedly to celebrate International Women's Year. An IWY conference was held in each of the 50 states, culminating with a national convention in Houston in November 1977. Every feminist of any fame was a participant in this Conference, including Gloria Steinem, Betty Friedan, Eleanor Smeal, and Bella Abzug, who was the chairman.

The conferences were all run as forums promoting ERA and the feminist agenda. Only pro-ERA speakers were permitted on the platforms of the 50 state conferences and the Houston national conference. The media coverage was immense, and the Houston platform was graced by three First Ladies: Rosalynn Carter, Betty Ford, and Ladybird Johnson.

At the IWY event in Houston, the ERAers, the abortionists, and the lesbians made the decision to march in unison for their common goals. The conference enthusiastically passed what the media called the "hot button" issues: ERA, abortion and abortion funding, and lesbian and gay rights. The IWY Conference doomed ERA because it showed the television audience that ERA and the feminist movement were outside the mainstream of America. ERA never passed anywhere in the post-IWY period.

ERA Referenda

The ERA advocates tried to blame the defeat of ERA on a few men in several state legislatures. But when ERA was submitted to a vote of the people it nearly always lost. The voters in the following seven states rejected ERA in statewide referenda. (Nevada was an advisory referendum on the Federal ERA; the others were State ERA referenda.) Wisconsin - 11/1973 (60,000 majority against), New York - 11/1975 (420,000 majority against), New Jersey - 11/1975 (52% against), Nevada 11/1978 (66% against), Florida 11/1978 (60% against), Iowa 11/1980 (55% against), and Maine 11/1984 (64% against).

ERA Time Extension

The original ERA resolution which passed Congress on March 22, 1972 included the following preamble preceding the three sections of the text of ERA:

"Resolved by the Senate and House of Representatives of the United States of America in Congress assembled (two-thirds of each House concurring therein), that the following article is proposed as an amendment to the Constitution of the United States, which shall be valid to all intents and purposes as part of the Constitution when ratified by the legislatures of three-fourths of the several States within seven years from the date of its submission by the Congress:

"Section 1: Equality of rights under the law shall not be denied or abridged by the United States or by any State on account of sex.

"Section 2: The Congress shall have the power to enforce, by appropriate legislation, the provisions of this article.

"Section 3: This amendment shall take effect two years after the date of ratification."

When the end of the seven years approached and it became clear that three-fourths of the states (38 states) would not ratify ERA, Congress passed an ERA Time Extension resolution to change "within seven years" to 10 years, 3 months, 8 days, 7 hours and 35 minutes, so that the time limit was extended to June 30,1982 (instead of expiring on March 22, 1979).

In an additional piece of chicanery, Congress passed the ERA Time Extension by only a simple majority vote instead of by the two-thirds majority vote required by Article V of the U.S. Constitution for all constitutional amendments.

The ERA advocates' strategy of a Time Extension was to lock in all those states which had ratified in 1972 and 1973, while money and media were concentrated on ratification efforts in the non-ratified states where they thought ERA had the best chance (in this order): Illinois, Florida, North Carolina, Oklahoma, Georgia, and Virginia. This ratification effort was assisted by a boycott of all states that had not ratified ERA, designed particularly to cause economic harm to the convention cities in the unratified states.

The American people were so turned off by the unfairness of the Time Extension—and the refusal of the ERA proponents to recognize the legality of the rescissions—that not a single state ratified ERA after the Time Extension was passed by Congress in 1978.

After a two-and-a-half-year lawsuit, the U.S. District Court ruled on December 23, 1981 in Idaho v. Freeman that the ERA Time Extension voted by Congress was unconstitutional and that the rescissions of ERA were constitutional. The U.S. Supreme Court did not decide the appeal of this case until after the expiration of ERA on June 30, 1982, at which time the Supreme Court ruled that the case was moot and no longer needed to be decided.

Despite the Time Extension, the ERA opponents held a big dinner in Washington, D.C., called "The End of an ERA," on March 22, 1979, to celebrate the constitutional termination of ERA. This was the end of the seven-year time limit set by Congress when ERA was sent to the states in 1972.

As a practical matter, March 22, 1979 was not the end of ERA—since the unfair Time Extension forced three more years of emotional battles in many state legislatures. But March 22, 1979 was truly "the end of an era"—the end of the era of conservative defeats.

Up until that time, conservatives had lost so many battles that they had a defeatist attitude. The proclaimed victory over ERA showed the conservatives and pro-family activists that they could win an important political battle—despite overwhelming odds and the opposition of nearly all the media and most elected officials at every level of government. Since 1979, the conservatives and pro-family movement have had an unbroken series of victories,

highlighted by the election and landslide reelection of Ronald
Reagan.

On June 30, 1982, the ERA opponents held a second
"burial" of the ERA at a large dinner in Washington called "The
Rainbow Dinner." On that day, no one could deny the fact that the
proposed federal ERA was truly dead.

ERA Tries in Congress Again

In January 1983, the ERA advocates re-introduced ERA into
the U.S. Congress with the full support of Speaker Tip O'Neill. After
a year of intensive lobbying, ERA came to a vote in the House on
November 15,1983, and 147 Congressmen voted no. That was six
votes short of the two-thirds majority required to send ERA out to
the states again.

What killed ERA in 1983 was the House Judiciary "markup"
on November 9, an all-day session with 5-1/2 hours of calm and
rational debate. No television lights were on, so no one was
posturing for the media. Nine amendments to ERA were offered in
that Committee. Although all nine were defeated, each of the nine
amendments received 12 or 13 "yes" votes. It is well known in
Washington that the Judiciary Committee is so liberal that any
motion which gets a dozen "yes" votes there is sure to win on the
House floor.

Rep. James Sensenbrenner's (R-WI) amendment would have
made ERA abortion-neutral. On October 20, 1983, the Congressional
Research Service had issued "a legal analysis of the potential impact

of ERA on abortion" and concluded on page 61 that "ERA would reach abortion and abortion funding situations." That would mean that ERA would invalidate the Hyde Amendment and mandate taxpayer-funding of abortions. The ERA advocates could not deny this effect, but they were unwilling to separate the ERA and abortion questions by voting for the Sensenbrenner amendment.

Rep. Sam Hall's (D-TX) amendment would have prevented ERA from drafting women. The opponents of the Hall amendment admitted that ERA would draft women just like men but argued that women want this kind of equality.

Rep. Clay Shaw (R-FL) offered an amendment to prevent ERA from requiring women to serve in military combat just like men. Rep. Patricia Schroeder (D-CO) argued that women deserve their career opportunities to serve in combat just like men.

Rep. George Gekas (R-PA) offered an amendment to prevent ERA from wiping out veterans' preference. At the House Judiciary Committee hearing on September 14, 1983, League of Women Voters President Dorothy S. Ridings had testified that ERA would outlaw veterans' preference by overturning the 1979 Supreme Court case of Massachusetts v. Feeney. Both the Veterans of Foreign Wars and the American Legion objected to this effect.

Rep. Harold Sawyer (R-MI) offered an amendment to prevent ERA from wiping out the ability of insurance companies to charge lower insurance rates to women for automobile accident and life insurance policies. The ERA advocates admit that one of their goals is to force all insurance to be "unisex" regardless of accident and actuarial tables.

Rep. Tom Kindness (R-OH) offered an amendment to put the seven-year time limit on ERA in the text of the Amendment instead of in the preamble (in order to prevent another constitutional dispute about a time extension). Then he offered another amendment to give the states concurrent enforcement power, as well as the Federal Government. The ERA advocates opposed both purposes.

The biggest surprise of the day was the amendment offered by Rep. Dan Lungren (R-CA) to exempt religious schools from the effect of ERA. This amendment was made necessary by the 1983 Supreme Court decision in Bob Jones University v. United States, which ruled that the Internal Revenue Service can withdraw tax exemption from any school operated by a church which has any regulation contrary to public policy.

If ERA means anything at all, it means a "public policy" against sex discrimination. So, if the ruling of the Bob Jones case were applied under ERA, the result almost certainly would be that all religious schools run by churches and synagogues that do not ordain women, or which treat men and women differently, would lose their tax exemption. Thus, ERA would put at risk the tax exemption of thousands of Catholic, Protestant, and Jewish schools all over the country. Most Congressmen are not willing to tell their constituents that religious schools will lose their tax exemption.

At the end of the day, the diehard ERAers went crying to Speaker O'Neill, imploring him to devise a way to prevent these nine amendments from being offered on the House floor.

So, Speaker O'Neill brought ERA to a vote of the House on November 15, 1983 under a procedure called "suspension of the

14

rules." This meant that no amendments of any kind could be offered. In a dramatic roll call, ERA lost by a six-vote margin.

This vote made it clear that Congress will never pass ERA. Politically, it is as dead as the Prohibition Amendment.

The Effort for State ERAs

At the same time that the ERA advocates were trying again in Congress in 1983, they sought to rebuild their momentum through a series of state ERAs.

In Wisconsin, the state legislators tried to assist this project by adding to the text of the proposed state ERA some additional language that would prevent it from being used to mandate abortion funding or gay rights. To the amazement of those legislators, the leading ERA advocates (including the National Organization for Women, the League of Women Voters, and the American Civil Liberties Union) publicly opposed ERA in this form, and so the Wisconsin ERA died. This experience makes it clear that the ERA advocates want ERA primarily, and perhaps solely, to achieve abortion funding and gay rights.

A similar scenario took place in Minnesota. After a state ERA was proposed in the spring of 1983, a committee added a section to make it abortion-neutral. The next day the ERA sponsor withdrew ERA. The ERA advocates obviously do not want ERA unless it includes their hidden agenda.

ERA advocates then chose Maine as the most advantageous state to "start the ball rolling" for ERA again. They had the full

15

support of the media, all public officials of both parties, and a cooperative legislature which passed ERA without the encumbrance of any additional language. The referendum to add a state ERA to Maine's constitution took place on November 6, 1984. When the votes were counted, 64 percent of the people had voted "no."

Chapter 2
What's Wrong With "Equal Rights" for Women?
February 1972

O f all the classes of people who ever lived, the American woman is the most privileged. We have the most rights and rewards, and the fewest duties. Our unique status is the result of a fortunate combination of circumstances.

First, we have the immense good fortune to live in a civilization which respects the family as the basic unit of society. This respect is part and parcel of our laws and our customs. It is based on the fact of life—which no legislation or agitation can erase—that women have babies and men don't.

If you don't like this fundamental difference, you will have to take up your complaint with God because He created us this way. The fact that women, not men, have babies is not the fault of selfish and domineering men, or of the establishment, or of any clique of conspirators who want to oppress women. It's simply the way God made us.

Our Judeo-Christian civilization has developed the law and custom that, since women must bear the physical consequences of the sex act, men must be required to bear the other consequences and pay in other ways. These laws and customs decree that a man must carry his share by physical protection and financial support of his children and of the woman who bears his children, and also by a code of behavior which benefits and protects both the woman and the children.

The Greatest Achievement of Women's Rights

This is accomplished by the institution of the family. Our respect for the family as the basic unit of society, which is ingrained in the laws and customs of our Judeo-Christian civilization, is the greatest single achievement in the entire history of women's rights. It assures a woman the most precious and important right of all—the right to keep her own baby and to be supported and protected in the enjoyment of watching her baby grow and develop.

The institution of the family is advantageous for women for many reasons. After all, what do we want out of life? To love and be loved? Mankind has not discovered a better nest for a lifetime of reciprocal love. A sense of achievement? A man may search 30 to 40 years for accomplishment in his profession. A woman can enjoy real achievement when she is young—by having a baby. She can have the satisfaction of doing a job well—and being recognized for it.

Do we want financial security? We are fortunate to have the great legacy of Moses, the Ten Commandments, especially this one: "Honor thy father and thy mother that thy days may be long upon the land." Children are a woman's best social security—her best guarantee of social benefits such as old age pension, unemployment compensation, workman's compensation, and sick leave. The family gives a woman the physical, financial and emotional security of the home—for all her life.

The Financial Benefits of Chivalry

The second reason why American women are a privileged group is that we are the beneficiaries of a tradition of special respect for women which dates from the Christian Age of Chivalry. The honor and respect paid to Mary, the Mother of Christ, resulted in all women, in effect, being put on a pedestal.

This respect for women is not just the lip service that politicians pay to "God, Motherhood, and the Flag." It is not—as some youthful agitators seem to think—just a matter of opening doors for women, seeing that they are seated first, carrying their bundles, and helping them in and out of automobiles. Such good manners are merely the superficial evidences of a total attitude toward women which expresses itself in many more tangible ways, such as money.

In other civilizations, such as the African and the American Indian, the men strut around wearing feathers and beads and hunting and fishing (great sport for men!), while the women do all the hard, tiresome drudgery including the tilling of the soil (if any is done), the hewing of wood, the making of fires, the carrying of water, as well as the cooking, sewing and caring for babies.

This is not the American way because we were lucky enough to inherit the traditions of the Age of Chivalry. In America, a man's first significant purchase is a diamond for his bride, and the largest financial investment of his life is a home for her to live in.

American husbands work hours of overtime to buy a fur piece or other finery to keep their wives in fashion, and to pay premiums on their life insurance policies to provide for her comfort when she is a widow (benefits in which he can never share).

In the states which follow the English common law, a wife has a dower right in her husband's real estate which he cannot take away from her during life or by his will. A man cannot dispose of his real estate without his wife's signature. Any sale is subject to her 1/3 interest.

Women fare even better in the states which follow the Spanish and French community-property laws, such as California, Arizona, Texas and Louisiana. The basic philosophy of the Spanish/French law is that a wife's work in the home is just as valuable as a husband's work at his job. Therefore, in community-property states, a wife owns one-half of all the property and income her husband earns during their marriage, and he cannot take it away from her.

In Illinois, as a result of agitation by "equal rights" fanatics, the real-estate dower laws were repealed as of January 1, 1972. This means that in Illinois a husband can now sell the family home, spend the money on his girlfriend or gamble it away, and his faithful wife of 30 years can no longer stop him. "Equal rights" fanatics have also deprived women in Illinois and in some other states of most of their basic common-law rights to recover damages for breach of promise to marry, seduction, criminal conversation, and alienation of affections.

The Real Liberation of Women

The third reason why American women are so well off is that the great American free enterprise system has produced remarkable inventors who have lifted the backbreaking "women's work" from our shoulders.

In other countries and in other eras, it was truly said that "Man may work from sun to sun, but woman's work is never done." Other women have labored every waking hour—preparing food on wood-burning stoves, making flour, baking bread in stone ovens, spinning yam, making clothes, making soap, doing the laundry by hand, heating irons, making candles for light and fires for warmth, and trying to nurse their babies through illnesses without medical care.

The real liberation of women from the backbreaking drudgery of centuries is the American free enterprise system which stimulated inventive geniuses to pursue their talents—and we all reap the profits. The great heroes of women's liberation are not the straggly-haired women on television talk shows and picket lines, but Thomas Edison who brought the miracle of electricity to our homes to give light and to run all those labor-saving devices—the equivalent, perhaps, of a half-dozen household servants for every middle-class American woman. Or Elias Howe who gave us the sewing machine which resulted in such an abundance of readymade clothing. Or Clarence Birdseye who invented the process for freezing foods. Or Henry Ford, who mass-produced the automobile so that it is within the price-range of every American, man or woman.

A major occupation of women in other countries is doing their daily shopping for food, which requires carrying their own containers and standing in line at dozens of small shops. They buy only small portions because they can't carry very much and have no refrigerator or freezer to keep a surplus anyway. Our American free enterprise system has given us the gigantic food and packaging industry and beautiful supermarkets, which provide an endless variety of foods, prepackaged for easy carrying and a minimum of waiting. In America, women have the freedom from the slavery of standing in line for daily food. Thus, household duties have been reduced to only a few hours a day, leaving the American woman with plenty of time to moonlight. She can take a full or part-time paying job, or she can indulge to her heart's content in a tremendous selection of interesting educational or cultural or homemaking activities.

The Fraud of The Equal Rights Amendment

In the last couple of years, a noisy movement has sprung up agitating for "women's rights." Suddenly, everywhere we are afflicted with aggressive females on television talk shows yapping about how mistreated American women are, suggesting that marriage has put us in some kind of "slavery," that housework is menial and degrading, and—perish the thought—that women are discriminated against. New "women's liberation" organizations are popping up, agitating and demonstrating, serving demands on public officials, getting wide press coverage always, and purporting to speak for some 100,000,000 American women.

It's time to set the record straight. The claim that American women are downtrodden and unfairly treated is the fraud of the century. The truth is that American women never had it so good. Why should we lower ourselves to "equal rights" when we already have the status of special privilege?

The proposed Equal Rights Amendment states: "Equality of rights under the law shall not be denied or abridged by the United States or by any state on account of sex." So, what's wrong with that? Well, here are a few examples of what's wrong with it.

This Amendment will absolutely and positively make women subject to the draft. Why any woman would support such a ridiculous and un-American proposal as this is beyond comprehension. Why any Congressman who had any regard for his wife, sister or daughter would support such a proposition is just as hard to understand. Foxholes are bad enough for men, but they certainly are not the place for women—and we should reject any proposal which would put them there in the name of "equal rights."

It is amusing to watch the semantic chicanery of the advocates of the Equal Rights Amendment when confronted with this issue of the draft. They evade, they sidestep, they try to muddy up the issue, but they cannot deny that the Equal Rights Amendment will positively make women subject to the draft. Congresswoman Margaret Heckler's answer to this question was, don't worry, it will take two years for the Equal Rights Amendment to go into effect, and we can rely on President Nixon to end the Vietnam War before then!

Literature distributed by Equal Rights Amendment supporters confirms that "under the Amendment a draft law which applied to men would apply also to women." The Equal Rights literature argues that this would be good for women so they can achieve their "equal rights" in securing veterans' benefits.

Another bad effect of the Equal Rights Amendment is that it will abolish a woman's right to child support and alimony, and substitute what the women's libbers think is a more "equal" policy, that "such decisions should be within the discretion of the Court and should be made on the economic situation and need of the parties in the case."

Under present American laws, the man is always required to support his wife and each child he caused to be brought into the world. Why should women abandon these good laws—by trading them for something so nebulous and uncertain as the "discretion of the Court?"

The law now requires a husband to support his wife as best as his financial situation permits, but a wife is not required to support her husband (unless he is about to become a public charge). A husband cannot demand that his wife go to work to help pay for family expenses. He has the duty of financial support under our laws and customs. Why should we abandon these mandatory wife-support and child-support laws so that a wife would have an "equal" obligation to take a job?

By law and custom in America, in case of divorce, the mother always is given custody of her children unless there is overwhelming evidence of mistreatment, neglect or bad character. This is our special privilege because of the high rank that is placed on motherhood in our society. Do women really want to give up this special privilege and lower themselves to "equal rights," so that the mother gets one child and the father gets the other? I think not.

The Right NOT To Take A Job

Passage of the Equal Rights Amendment would open up a Pandora's box of trouble for women. It would deprive the American woman of many of the fundamental special privileges we now enjoy, and especially the greatest rights of all: (1) NOT to take a job, (2) to keep her baby, and (3) to be supported by her husband.

How have the proponents of the Equal Rights Amendment been so successful that it passed the House of Representatives in 1971 by a large margin? There are three reasons. First, most people mistakenly believe that "equal rights" means simply "equal pay for equal work," and we are all in favor of this. But this goal has already been practically achieved by legislation, and the remaining violations can also be wiped out by legislation. Only 12 states still have obsolete discriminatory laws.

Second, Equal Rights Amendment literature lists many women's organizations as supporters. Most of these organizations probably gave their endorsement after being told that this Amendment will bring better jobs and more pay for women but were never told what basic rights women would give up. That is the way, for example, that it happened at the October 1971 Convention of the National Federation of Republican Women, where the tight little clique running things from the top presented speaker after speaker to promote the Equal Rights Amendment, but gave no "equal rights" to delegates who wanted to speak against it. The 1971 officers of the NFRW even published intemperate attacks on the Republican Congressmen who voted for an amendment to the Equal Rights Amendment which would exempt women from the draft and permit states to enact "reasonable" laws based on sex differences.

Thirdly, the women's lib agitators caught the Congressmen badly off-guard and they felt they could not risk being labeled "anti-women." The Congressmen simply didn't hear from the millions of happily married women who believe in the laws which protect the family and require the husband to support his wife and children. They only heard from the few but noisy unhappy women.

Equal Rights in Russia

At women's lib rallies, some of the fiery speakers cite Russia as an example of a country where women have equal rights. The Soviet Constitution guarantees, "Woman in the U.S.S.R. is accorded equal rights with men in all spheres of economic, state, cultural, public and political life."

"Equal rights" in the Soviet Union means that the Russian woman is obliged to put her baby in a state-operated nursery or kindergarten so she can join the labor force. Under Soviet law, a woman (as well as a man) can be jailed for refusing to engage in "socially useful labor" or for leading a "parasitic way of life."

"Equal rights" in Russia means that the women do the heavy, dirty work American women do not do—but men are still the bosses. Russian women have "equal rights" to mine coal, load cargo ships, work in heavy construction, and labor in the fields. A typical garbage pickup team consists of two women hauling the garbage and a man driving the truck. A typical road construction "brigade" consists of a dozen women digging ditches while a male "brigadier" supervises. Of course, the women still do all the housework (without electrical appliances) and all the standing in line to buy food for their families.

A Russian woman journalist recently wrote in a report called "Unbearable Burden," about women's employment in heavy construction work that, "The years given over to a 'male' occupation can rob her of the main thing: her happiness as a woman, the joy of motherhood." Abortions are available for the asking and the average Russian woman has had several, while limiting herself to one or two children. Under Soviet-style "equal rights," the men still hold all the top jobs. Nine out of every ten plant managers are men. Three out of four school principals are men. There is no woman member in the all-powerful Politburo or Party Secretariat.

What "Women's Lib" Really Means

Many women are under the mistaken impression that "women's lib" means more job employment opportunities for women, equal pay for equal work, appointments of women to high positions, admitting more women to medical schools, and other desirable objectives which all women favor. We all support these purposes, as well as any necessary legislation which would bring them about.

But all this is only a sweet syrup which covers the deadly poison masquerading as "women's lib." The women's libbers are radicals who are waging a total assault on the family, on marriage, and on children. Don't take my word for it—read their own literature and prove to yourself what these characters are trying to do.

The most pretentious of the women's liberation magazines is called *Ms.*, and subtitled "The New Magazine For Women," with Gloria Steinem listed as president and secretary.

Reading the Spring 1972 issue of *Ms.* gives a good understanding of women's lib, and the people who promote it. It is anti-family, anti-children, and pro-abortion. It is a series of sharp-tongued, high-pitched whining complaints by unmarried women. They view the home as a prison, and the wife and mother as a slave. To these women's libbers, marriage means dirty dishes and dirty laundry. One article lauds a woman's refusal to carry up the family laundry as "an act of extreme courage." Another tells how satisfying it is to be a lesbian.

The women's libbers don't understand that most women want to be wife, mother and homemaker—and are happy in that role. The women's libbers actively resent the mother who stays at home with her children and likes it that way. The principal purpose of *Ms.*'s shrill tirade is to sow seeds of discontent among happy, married women so that all women can be unhappy in some new sisterhood of frustrated togetherness.

Obviously intrigued by the 170 clauses of exemptions from marital duties given to Jackie Kennedy, and the special burdens imposed on Aristotle Onassis, in the pre-marriage contract they signed. *Ms.* recommends two women's lib marriage contracts. The "utopian marriage contract" has a clause on "sexual rights and freedoms" which approves "arrangements such as having Tuesdays off from one another," and the husband giving "his consent to abortion in advance."

The "Shulmans' marriage agreement" includes such petty provisions as "wife strips beds, husband remakes them," and "Husband does dishes on Tuesday, Thursday and Sunday. Wife does Monday, Wednesday and Saturday, Friday is split…" If the baby cries in the night, the chore of "handling" the baby is assigned as follows: "Husband does Tuesday, Thursday and Sunday. Wife does Monday, Wednesday and Saturday, Friday is split…" Presumably, if the baby cries for his mother on Tuesday night, he would be informed that the marriage contract prohibits her from answering.

Of course, it is possible, in such a loveless home, that the baby would never call for his mother at all.

Who put up the money to launch this 130-page slick-paper assault on the family and motherhood? A count of the advertisements in *Ms.* shows that the principal financial backer is the liquor industry. There are 26 liquor ads in this one initial issue. Of these, 13 are expensive full-page color ads, as opposed to only 18 full-page ads from all other sources combined, most of which are in the cheaper black-and-white.

Another women's lib magazine, called *Women*, tells the American woman that she is a prisoner in the "solitary confinement" and "isolation" of marriage. The magazine promises that it will provide women with "escape from isolation...release from boredom," and that it will "break the barriers...that separate wife, mistress and secretary...heterosexual women and homosexual women."

These women's libbers do, indeed, intend to "break the barriers" of the Ten Commandments and the sanctity of the family. It hasn't occurred to them that a woman's best "escape from isolation and boredom" is not a magazine subscription to boost her "stifled ego" but a husband and children who love her.

The first issue of *Women* contains 68 pages of such proposals as "The BITCH Manifesto," which promotes the line that "Bitch is Beautiful and that we have nothing to lose. Nothing whatsoever." Another article promotes an organization called W.I.T.C.H. (Women's International Terrorist Conspiracy from Hell), "an action arm of Women's Liberation."

In intellectual circles, a New York University professor named Warren T. Farrell has provided the rationale for why men should support women's lib. When his speech to the American Political Science Association Convention is stripped of its egghead verbiage, his argument is that men should eagerly look forward to the day when they can enjoy free sex and not have to pay for it. The husband will no longer be "saddled with the tremendous guilt feelings" when he leaves his wife with nothing after she has given him her best years. If a husband loses his job, he will no longer feel compelled to take any job to support his family. A husband can go "out with the boys" to have a drink without feeling guilty. Alimony will be eliminated.

Women's Libbers Do NOT Speak For Us

The "women's lib" movement is not an honest effort to secure better jobs for women who want or need to work outside the home. This is just the superficial sweet-talk to win broad support for a radical "movement." Women's lib is a total assault on the role of the American woman as wife and mother, and on the family as the basic unit of society.

Women's libbers are trying to make wives and mothers unhappy with their career, make them feel that they are "second-class citizens" and "abject slaves." Women's libbers are promoting free sex instead of the "slavery" of marriage. They are promoting Federal "day-care centers" for babies instead of homes. They are promoting abortions instead of families.

Why should we trade in our special privileges and honored status for the alleged advantage of working in an office or assembly line? Most women would rather cuddle a baby than a typewriter or factory machine. Most women find that it is easier to get along with a husband than a foreman or office manager. Offices and factories require many more menial and repetitive chores than washing dishing and ironing shirts.

Women's libbers do not speak for the majority of American women. American women do not want to be liberated from husbands and children. We do not want to trade our birthright of the special privileges of American women—for the mess of pottage called the Equal Rights Amendment.

Modern technology and opportunity have not discovered any nobler or more satisfying or more creative career for a woman than marriage and motherhood. The wonderful advantage that American women have is that we can have all the rewards of that number-one career, and still moonlight with a second one to suit our intellectual, cultural or financial tastes or needs.

And why should the men acquiesce in a system which gives preferential rights and lighter duties to women? In return, the men get the pearl of great price: a happy home, a faithful wife, and children they adore.

If the women's libbers want to reject marriage and motherhood, it's a free country and that is their choice. But let's not permit these women's libbers to get away with pretending to speak for the rest of us. Let's not permit this tiny minority to degrade the role that most women prefer. Let's not let these women's libbers deprive wives and mothers of the rights we now possess.

Tell your Senators NOW that you want them to vote NO on the Equal Rights Amendment. Tell your television and radio stations that you want equal time to present the case FOR marriage and motherhood.

Chapter 3
The Fraud Called the Equal Rights Amendment
May 1972

I f there ever was an example of how a tiny minority can cram its views down the throats of the majority, it is the Equal Rights Amendment, called ERA. A noisy claque of women's lib agitators rammed ERA through Congress, intimidating the men into voting for it so they would not be labeled "anti-woman."

The ERA passed Congress with big majorities on March 22, 1972 and was sent to the states for ratification. When it is ratified by 38 states, it will become the law of the land. Within two hours of Senate passage, Hawaii ratified it. New Hampshire and Nebraska, both anxious to be second, rushed their approval the next day. Then in steady succession came Iowa, Idaho, Delaware, Kansas, Texas, Maryland, Tennessee, Alaska, Rhode Island, and New Jersey. As this goes to press, 13 states have ratified it and others are on the verge of doing so.

Three states have rejected it: Oklahoma, Vermont and Connecticut.

What is ERA? The Amendment reads: "Equality of rights under the law shall not be denied or abridged by the United States or by any state on account of sex."

Does that sound good? Don't kid yourself. This innocuous-sounding amendment will take away far more important rights than it will ever give. This was made abundantly clear by the debate in Congress. Senator Sam Ervin (D., N.C.) called it "the most drastic measure in Senate history." He proved this by putting into the Congressional Record an article from the Yale Law Journal of April 1971.

The importance of this Yale Law Journal article is that both the proponents and the opponents of ERA agree that it is an accurate analysis of the consequences of ERA. Congresswoman Martha Griffiths, a leading proponent of ERA, sent a copy of this article to every member of Congress, stating that "It will help you understand the purposes and effects of the Equal Rights Amendment...The article explains how the ERA will work in most areas of the law."

Another leading supporter of ERA, Senator Birch Bayh, inserted a copy of the Yale Law Journal article in the Congressional Record, declaring it to be a "masterly piece of scholarship."

Senator Sam Ervin, the leading opponent of ERA, agrees that the Yale Law Journal article is accurate. It is probably the definitive analysis of what the consequences will be. The following quotations are from this Yale Law Journal article and are identified as YLJ.

1. ERA will wipe out the financial obligation of a husband and father to support his wife and children—the most important of all women's rights.

"In all states husbands are primarily liable for the support of their wives and children…The child support sections of the criminal nonsupport laws…could not be sustained where only the male is liable for support." (YLJ, pp. 944-945)

"The Equal Rights Amendment would bar a state from imposing greater liability for support on a husband than on a wife merely because of his sex." (YLJ, p. 945)

"Like the duty of support during marriage and the obligation to pay alimony in the case of separation or divorce, nonsupport would have to be eliminated as a ground for divorce against husbands only." (YLJ, p .951)

"The Equal Rights Amendment would not require that alimony be abolished but only that it be available equally to husbands and wives." (YLJ, p. 952)

2. ERA will wipe out the laws which protect only women against sex crimes such as rape.

"Courts faced with criminal laws which do not apply equally to men and women would be likely to invalidate the laws rather than extending or rewriting them to apply to women and men alike." (YLJ, p. 966)

"Seduction laws, statutory rape laws, laws prohibiting obscene language in the presence of women, prostitution and 'manifest danger' laws…The Equal Rights Amendment would not permit such laws, which base their sex discriminatory classification on social stereotypes." (YLJ, p. 954)

"The statutory rape laws, which punish men for having sexual intercourse with any woman under an age specified by law...suffer from a double defect under the Equal Rights Amendment." (YLJ, p. 957)

"To be sure, the singling out of women probably reflects sociological reality...But the Equal Rights Amendment forbids finding legislative justification in the sexual double standard." (YLJ, p. 958)

"Just as the Equal Rights Amendment would invalidate prostitution laws which apply to women only, so the ERA would require invalidation of laws specially designed to protect women from being forced into prostitution." (YLJ, p. 964)

"A court would probably resolve doubts about Congressional intent by striking down the [Federal White Slave Traffic—Mann Act]." (YLJ, p. 965)

3. ERA will make women subject to the draft and to combat duty equally with men.

"The Equal Rights Amendment will have a substantial and pervasive impact upon military practices and institutions. As now formulated, the Amendment permits no exceptions for the military." (YLJ, p. 969)

"Women will serve in all kinds of units, and they will be eligible for combat duty. The double standard for treatment of sexual activity of men and women will be prohibited." (YLJ, p. 978)

"Neither the right to privacy nor any unique physical characteristic justifies different treatment of the sexes with respect to voluntary or involuntary service, and pregnancy justifies only slightly different conditions of service for women." (YLJ, p. 969)

"Such obvious differential treatment for women as exemption from the draft, exclusion from the service academies, and more restrictive standards for enlistment will have to be brought into conformity with the Amendment's basic prohibition of sex discrimination." (YLJ, p. 969)

"These changes will require a radical restructuring of the military's view of women." (YLJ, p. 969.)

"The Equal Rights Amendment will greatly hasten this process and will require the military to see women as it sees men." (YLJ, p. 970)

"A woman will register for the draft at the age of eighteen, as a man now does." (YLJ, p. 971)

"Under the Equal Rights Amendment, all standards applied through [intelligence tests and physical examinations] will have to be neutral as between the sexes." (YLJ, p. 971)

"Height standards will have to be revised from the dual system which now exists." (YLJ, p. 971)

"The height-weight correlations for the sexes will also have to be modified." (YLJ, p. 972)

"[Deferment policy] could provide that one, but not both, of the parents would be deferred. For example, whichever parent was called first might be eligible for service; the remaining parent, male or female, would be deferred." (YLJ, p. 973)

"If the rules continue to require discharge of women with dependent children, then men in a similar situation will also have to be discharged...The nondiscriminatory alternative is to allow both men and women with children to remain in the service and to take their dependents on assignments in noncombat zones, as men are now permitted to do." (YLJ, p. 975)

"Distinctions between single and married women who become pregnant will be permissible only if the same distinction is drawn between single and married men who father children." (YLJ, p. 975)

"Thus, if unmarried women are discharged for pregnancy, men shown to be fathers of children born out of wedlock would also be discharged. Even in this form such a rule would be suspect under the Amendment, because it would probably be enforced more frequently against women. A court will therefore be likely to strike down the rule despite the neutrality of its terms, because of its differential impact." (YLJ, p. 975)

"Women are physically as able as men to perform many jobs classified as combat duty, such as piloting an airplane or engaging in naval operations...There is no reason to prevent women from doing these jobs in combat zones." (YLJ, p. 977)

"No one would suggest that...women who serve can avoid the possibility of physical harm and assault. But it is important to remember that all combat is dangerous, degrading and dehumanizing." (YLJ, p. 977)

4. ERA will wipe out the right of the mother to keep her children in case of divorce.

"In 90 percent of custody cases the mother is awarded the custody. The Equal Rights Amendment would prohibit both statutory and common law presumptions about which parent was the proper guardian based on the sex of the parent." (YLJ, p. 953)

5. ERA will lower the age at which boys can marry.

"Physical capacity to bear children can no longer justify a different statutory marriage age for men and women." (YLJ, p. 939)

6. ERA will wipe out the protections women now have from dangerous and unpleasant jobs.

"There is little reason to doubt, therefore, that courts will invalidate weightlifting regulations for women under the Equal Rights Amendment." (YLJ, p. 935)

"States which grant jury service exemption to women with children will either extend the exemption to men with children or abolish the exemption altogether." (YLJ, p. 920)

A librarian at the University of California Library, Mrs. Laurel Burley, has made a deep study of the drastic consequences of ERA on labor laws which provide advantages for working-class women. She states that, "The major danger in the proposed ERA lies in the fact that it would in one fell swoop invalidate all protective legislation enacted by the States to protect working women from exploitative employers…Protective legislation not only sets maximum hours and minimum wage standards, but also mandates such provisions as rest areas, toilet facilities, elevators, adequate lighting and ventilation, rest and meal breaks (including the right to eat one's meal away from the immediate work area), adequate drinking water (important for women and children who are farm workers), and protective garments and uniforms." (Congressional Record, March 22, 1972, p. S4577)

7. ERA will wipe out women's right to privacy.

Professor Paul Freund of the Harvard Law School testified that ERA would be absolute and "would require that there be no segregation of the sexes in prison, reform schools, public restrooms, and other public facilities."

Professor Phil Kurland, Editor of the Supreme Court Review and a Professor of Law at the University of Chicago Law School, testified before the Senate Judiciary Committee, and here is the colloquy:

"*Senator Ervin.* The law which exists in North Carolina and in virtually every other state of the Union which requires separate restrooms for boys and girls in public schools would be nullified, would it not?

"*Professor Kurland.* That is right, unless the separate but equal doctrine is revived.

"*Senator Ervin.* And the laws of the states and the regulations of the Federal government which require separate restrooms for men and women in public buildings would also be nullified, would it not?

"*Professor Kurland.* My answer would be the same."

Senator Ervin then concluded, "A few examples in our society where the privacy aspect of the relationship between men and women would be changed are: (1) Police practices by which a search involving the removal of clothing will be able to be performed by members of either sex without regard to the sex of the one to be searched. (2) Segregation by sex in sleeping quarters of prisons or similar public institutions would be outlawed. (3) Segregation by sex of living conditions in the armed forces would be outlawed. This includes close quarter living in combat zones and foxholes. (4) Segregation by sex in hospitals would be outlawed. (5) Physical exams in the armed forces will have to be carried out on a sex neutral basis." (Congressional Record, March 22, 1972, p. S4578)

Do Women Want ERA?

One of the great myths put over on the politicians is the illusion that American women want the Equal Rights Amendment. The majority certainly do not want ERA.

The only detailed poll ever taken on women's opinions on the ERA was done by Elmo Roper in September 1971.

In the Roper Poll, 77 percent of American women disagree "that women should have equal treatment regarding the draft." Yet, the Congressional debate and the Yale Law Journal article confirm that ERA will positively cause women to be drafted and to serve in combat.

In the Roper Poll, 83 percent of American women disagree that "a wife should be the breadwinner if a better wage earner than husband." Yet, the Congressional debate and the Yale Law Journal article confirm that ERA will eliminate a man's obligation to be the breadwinner and support his wife and children.

In the Roper Poll, 69 percent of American women disagree that "a divorced woman should pay alimony if she has money and her husband hasn't." Yet, the Congressional debate and the Yale Law Journal confirm that ERA will make women and men equally liable for alimony.

The February Phyllis Schlafly Report called "What's Wrong with Equal Rights For Women?" drew the biggest response in the five-year history of this newsletter. This is just additional confirmation of the fact that American women do not want to be reduced to the level of "equal rights."

On April 19, 1972, Phyllis Schlafly appeared on a one-hour television program called the Phil Donohue Show, aired in 42 cities. The live studio audience was 98 percent against women's lib and the Equal Rights Amendment.

Most interesting was the flood of fan mail which resulted from the show, also 98 percent against women's lib and the Equal Rights Amendment.

What Can You Do?

To abolish unreasonable and unfair discriminations against women is a worthy goal which can be achieved by specific legislation and by application of the Equal Protection Clause of the Constitution. To resort to the Equal Rights Amendment for this purpose is about as unwise as using an atomic bomb to exterminate mice.

The ERA will not promote women to better jobs, will not elect more women to public office, and will not convince men they should help with the housework. It will cause massive disruption of our military defense and chaos in our laws. Just think, for example, of the dislocations caused by the fact that ERA will "prohibit the states from requiring that a child's last name be the same as his or her father's." (YLJ, p. 941)

Most important, ERA will deprive the American woman of her most cherished right of all—the right to stay home, keep her baby, and be supported by her husband.

What can you do? Well, if you live in Hawaii, New Hampshire, Nebraska, Iowa, Idaho, Delaware, Kansas, Texas, Maryland, Tennessee, Alaska, Rhode Island, or New Jersey, you are too late to do anything. The women's libbers were too fast for you.

If you live in Oklahoma, Vermont or Connecticut, you can congratulate yourself that you have women who were ready for the battle when it was thrust upon them.

If you live in one of the other states, run, don't walk, to the home of your most effective and persuasive woman friend. Take this *Report* with you and discuss it with her.

Then, telephone your own state legislator. Find out if your State Legislature is in session. If it is, find out the days of the week that the legislators are in their offices at the State Capitol (usually Tuesdays and Wednesdays are the best). Then, you and your friend, and a couple of other women should go to the State Capitol and talk personally to every state legislator, using the arguments given in this Report. It would be best if you use these arguments as your own and in your own words, rather than giving them some piece of literature. You only need a handful of women to do the job because, remember, you are speaking for the majority. Good luck!

One more thing you can do is to use these arguments to request "equal time" on any television or radio program which presents the women's libbers or other advocates of the ERA. One of our readers successfully used the February Phyllis Schlafly Report to request equal time on the Phil Donohue Show. You can do this, too!

Chapter 4
Dear State Legislator: The Buck Stops With You
February 1973

Whether or not the proposed Equal Rights Amendment will become the 27th Amendment to the United States Constitution now depends on the State Legislators. The average State Legislator is a conscientious, hard-working family man or woman who wants to do the best thing for his or her constituents and is favorably inclined toward any legislation to benefit women.

When the average State Legislator is first confronted by the Equal Rights Amendment, he thinks to himself: Congress passed ERA by lopsided majorities, so who am I to get out on a limb with a negative vote?

Frank-talking U.S. Senators have been revealing the hitherto-hidden truth that they were unhappy about voting for ERA but did so simply to get themselves off the hook and to pass the buck to the State Legislatures. When asked why he voted for ERA, one prominent Republican Senator stated on May 8, 1972, "I voted for it to get those militant women off my back, and I figured I'd leave it up to the States to decide." *Washingtonian Magazine* quoted Senator Thomas Eagleton as admitting off the record that he and other members of Congress knew it was a bad piece of legislation but voted for it anyway.

In considering ratification of the Equal Rights Amendment, it is extremely important for State Legislators to realize that the House Judiciary Committee which voted out ERA did not approve ERA in its present form. The House Judiciary Committee approved the Equal Rights Amendment only with the attachment of the Wiggins Modification, which said:

"This article shall not impair the validity of any law of the United States which exempts a person from compulsory military service or any other law of the United States or of any State which reasonably promotes the health and safety of the people."

After the ERA-with-the-Wiggins-Modification reached the full House of Representatives, the Congressmen who had not heard the pro and con testimony caved in to the women's liberation lobbyists and struck out the Wiggins Modification. Then they passed ERA and sent it to the Senate, which passed it, too.

The Report of the House Judiciary Committee is extremely important because it proves that the majority of the Congressmen who held the hearings and heard the witnesses concluded that the Equal Rights Amendment by itself is very hurtful to women. Because this Report is so valuable to State Legislators, we reprint below significant passages from House Report No. 92-359:

"Danger of Judicial Chaos"

"During the course of your Committee's extensive deliberations on this proposal, thorough consideration was given to the record of the hearings conducted by Subcommittee No. 4 in March and April of this year, as well as to the lengthy legislative history of similar proposals in past years. That consideration has led us to the conclusion that, in the form in which it was introduced, House Joint Resolution 208 would create a substantial amount of confusion for our courts. To a large extent this confusion emanates from the fact that there is widespread disagreement among the proponents of the original text of House Joint Resolution 208 concerning its legal effects. These disagreements are so great as to create a substantial danger of judicial chaos if the original text is enacted.

"Although some of the proponents of the original language argue that the original text would permit both the Congress and State legislatures to make reasonable legal classifications into which sex is taken into account, other proponents argue strenuously that the use of the word 'equality' in the original text is intended to assure that men and women are given 'identical' legal treatment. In your Committee's view the latter construction would compel the courts to interpret the new Amendment as a mandate to sweep away all statutory sex distinctions per se. Such a per se rule would be undesirably rigid because it would leave no room to retain statutes which may reasonably reflect differences between the sexes.

"The rigidity of interpretation advocated by many of the proponents of the original text of House Joint Resolution 208 could produce a number of very undesirable results. For example, not only would women, including mothers, be subject to the draft but the military would be compelled to place them in combat units alongside of men. The same rigid interpretation could also require that work protective laws reasonably designed to protect the health and safety of women be invalidated; it could prohibit governmental financial assistance to such beneficial activities as summer camp programs in which boys are treated differently than girls; in some cases it could relieve the fathers of the primary responsibility for the support of even infant children, as well as the support of the mothers of such children and cast doubt on the validity of the millions of support decrees presently in existence. These are only a few examples of the undesirable effects that could be produced by the enactment of the original text of House Joint Resolution 208 [which is, of course, the present text of ERA now being considered by State Legislatures].

"To obviate the possibility of such effects and of judicial chaos, your Committee has recommended that the proposal be amended in such a way as to make it clear that Congress could exempt women from compulsory military service and that neither Congress nor State legislatures would be paralyzed from taking differences between the sexes into account when necessary to promote the health and safety of our people. This amendment to House Joint Resolution 208 is embodied in Committee Amendment No. 2 described above [which is the Wiggins Modification].

"The Committee Amendment No. 2 would avoid these pitfalls. It would, for example, allow us to retain reasonable laws designed to protect the health and safety of women, while striking down those laws based solely on sex that inhibit women in their efforts to seek gainful employment.

"Under the text of the proposed Constitutional Amendment as amended by your Committee, the courts would be directed to eliminate all unfair and irrational sex distinctions. Just as statutes classifying by race are subject to a very strict standard of equal protection scrutiny under the 14th Amendment, so too any State or Federal statute classifying by sex would likewise be subject to a strict standard of scrutiny under the proposed new Constitutional Amendment. Under such a strict standard a heavy burden would be placed on the State to show that any legal distinction between the sexes was compelled by some fundamental interest of the State in the health and safety of people. Yet while being strict the court could also apply rules of reason in those cases in which an overriding State interest relating to the draft or to health and safety calls for judicial recognition of the differences that do, in fact, exist between the sexes.

"In your Committee's view, the final effect of the Constitutional Amendment that we propose would accord with basic notions of fairness and with logic. The proposed Amendment would invalidate those invidious laws which discriminate improperly on the basis of sex. At the same time, however, it would permit us to retain those laws which realistically and rationally take sex into account and which equitably bring benefits to the majority of our citizens of both sexes.

"On June 22, 1971, the full Committee on the Judiciary approved House Joint Resolution 208 in executive session and ordered it favorably reported with amendments by a vote of 32 yeas, 3 nays." [This means that the Equal Rights Amendment with the Wiggins Modification was voted out of the Judiciary Committee by a vote of 32 to 3.]

"Who Is Bearing the Children?"

There were three House Judiciary Committee members who voted against the Equal Rights Amendment even with the Wiggins Modification because they believe that an Equal Rights Amendment in any form is hurtful to women. Here are some excerpts from Congressman Emanuel Celler's Minority Views:

"I stress we are dealing with a constitutional amendment. Every word thereof should have exacting scrutiny. It would be irresponsible to dismiss the language as a mere declaration of policy without consideration of the possible injurious effects that could flow therefrom. In all the swirling arguments and differing interpretations of the language of the proposal, there has been very little thought given to the triple role most women play in life, namely, that of wife, mother and worker. This is a heavy role indeed, and to wipe away the sustaining laws which help tip the scales in favor of women is to do injustice to millions of women who have chosen to marry, to make a home, to bear children, and to engage in gainful employment as well.

"For example, in most States the primary duty to support rests upon the husband. One possible effect of the Equal Rights Amendment would be to remove that primary legal obligation. The primary obligation to support is the foundation of the household. I refuse to allow the glad-sounding ring of an easy slogan to victimize millions of women and children. As one witness put it in hearings before the Committee, 'It is very doubtful that women would agree that a family support law is a curtailment of rights. Divorced, separated, or deserted wives struggling to support themselves and their children may find claims to support even harder to enforce than they are right now.'

"It has even been suggested by a proponent of the Equal Rights Amendment that the 'underlying social reality of the male as provider and the female as child bearer and rearer has changed.' May I, in turn, ask who is bearing the children and who is rearing them? As far as I know the Fallopian tube has not become vestigial.

"A host of questions would surround us should the Equal Rights Amendment be adopted which relate to State laws on the age of consent to marry, domicile, courtesy and dower rights, to cite but a few. These questions at this point are unanswerable. They become, with the adoption of this Amendment, litigable issues bringing the Federal courts into the delicate fabric of domestic relations.

"There will be no righting of wrongs if wrongfully done."

"Shifting Power to the Courts"

Here are some excerpts from Congressman Edward Hutchinson's Minority Views:

"Legislative power already exists to strike down every vestige of inequality between the sexes. A constitutional amendment is not needed either to create that power, to extend it, or to perfect it. If inequality between the sexes still exists in the law and public policy demands complete equality, then why not remove those inequalities legislatively?

"The proponents of a Constitutional Amendment answer that question by expressing their impatience with the piecemeal approach of the legislative process. They want to remove all inequality at one time by denying the power of government to recognize any inequality. But what they apparently fail to see is that they are simply trading one piecemeal approach for another. Instead of working with State legislatures and the Congress to write laws, amend laws, and repeal laws to remove such vestigial inequalities as yet remain, they will be suing in the courts to define the word equality, case by litigated case.

"All they will have accomplished is to change the forum, from the legislature to the courts. They will transfer the power to determine public policy in this important and rather fundamental area out of the legislative branch of government, the branch most directly responsive to the public will, and place it in the judiciary, the branch least responsive; and the Federal judiciary is not reachable by the people at all. My deep concern and, I trust, knowledge of the rightful

52

and proper relationship between the legislative and judicial functions persuade me that the public interest will be best served if the legislative power is not diminished and if the courts are not imposed upon to do the legislature's work of deciding public policy.

"Far different than enacting a statute which may be amended to reflect the changing times or to correct court interpretations of it, once Congress assents to the placing of language in the Constitution it puts that language beyond its reach. The language then becomes the tool of the Supreme Court to interpret it at will, and that Court has been known to find meanings and powers in Constitutional amendments undreamed of and unintended by the Congresses which proposed them and the State legislatures which ratified them. In the light of this history, Congress should painstakingly and exhaustively inquire into and even speculate upon all possible interpretations the Court may place upon the language if it would truly understand the scope of the restriction upon legislative power this proposed Amendment encompasses.

"The phrase 'Equality of rights under the law' will mean whatever the Supreme Court says it means, and that meaning may change from time to time as the membership of the Court changes. Within whatever meaning the Court may give that phrase, Congress is empowered by the second section of the article to make laws enforcing it.

"Without this Amendment, the States may legislate within the limits of the equal protection and due process clauses of the Fourteenth Amendment. With this Amendment, the states may not legislate at all on the subject of rights under the law, except as the Supreme Court may find their laws free of sexual inequality.

"A Revolutionary Change in the Family"

"It is not beyond the realm of possibility that the Court may find, sometime in the future, that by this Amendment, particularly the second section thereof, Congress was vested with power to take from the States the whole body of domestic relations law and perhaps part of their property law as well. These vast powers, further destroying the strength of our Federal system, would of course be exercisable by Congress only under the definitions given by the Court to the 'Equality of rights' phrase.

"The proponents say this Amendment will not reach nongovernmental action because the denial of equal rights is prohibited to the United States and any State. Under the Fourteenth Amendment only State action is prohibited, and still the Court has stretched the language to reach private covenants and trusts. The thing was accomplished by a holding that the courts could not be used to enforce such covenants and trusts. Similarly, under this Amendment the Court may hold that a private school for girls cannot use the courts to enforce its contracts, or that a testamentary trust cannot be set up wherein a father may direct the distribution of the corpus to his daughters at a different age than to his sons. Would the Court compel a private military school for boys to admit girls, or a summer camp for girls to take the boys along? I am satisfied that the Court would have no difficulty in extending this Constitutional

Amendment into the nongovernmental sector and will probably do so.

"The committee hearings confirm that one effect of this Constitutional Amendment would be to deny Congress the power to subject only men to the military draft. Some proponents argue that because women are not subject to the draft they are denied veterans benefits. This does not follow. Women may enlist in the military service, and those who join the military do so with all benefits accruing. The draft would bring women into the military against their will, and the hearings point out the difficulties and complexities which would spring from subjecting young mothers to the draft so long as young fathers are subject. The committee therefore amended the proposal to save Congress its present discretionary power over the draft. Of course, Congress has the present power to draft women but the proposal in its original form would compel Congress to draft women if men are drafted.

"The hearings also establish that there can be no inequality on account of sex in public institutions supported in whole or in part by governmental funds. The question of sexual segregation in prisons and penitentiaries, in educational institutions, and in medical and mental hospitals arises. Proponents say the requirement for equality of rights between the sexes will not destroy the right of privacy. I would hope they are right on that, but once the words are written into the Constitution it would be up to the courts to say. The right of privacy is not clear in the law at the present time. Until now it has been asserted only as a personal right. Could the legislative power make it a criminal offense to violate the segregation of sexes in institutions if consenting persons chose to waive their personal rights of privacy?

"Proponents want to leave all these policy decisions to the courts. I believe they should be left in the legislatures and in the Congress, and the way to leave them here is to defeat this Amendment.

"I am apprehensive the courts may in the future find within this Amendment Constitutional power to effect a revolutionary change in the institution of the family, a change to which I am opposed.

"Men and women are already equal under the law and I believe that whatever vestiges of inequality discriminatory against women still remain should be removed. I believe they can be removed legislatively and favor the legislature over the courts to accomplish that goal."

ERA "Quite Clearly" Drafts Women

Here are some excerpts from Congressman David W. Dennis' Minority Views:

"Again, the proposed Amendment, in its original form, quite clearly operates to subject women to the military draft. This would make for a fundamental change in American society which I would regard as highly undesirable and which, I am well satisfied, a clear majority of the American people does not desire.

"In like manner I see no good reason why Congress, or the Legislatures of the several States, should not retain full power to enact reasonable legislation to safeguard the health and safety of the people, including that reasonably designed to protect the health and safety of women."

"Women Must Serve On Combat Duty"

When the Equal Rights Amendment was reported out of the Senate Judiciary Committee, Senate Report No. 92-689 contained not only the comprehensive Minority Views of Senator Sam Ervin, Jr. (which have been quoted in previous issues of this newsletter), but also an important statement by Senator Hiram L. Fong. Here are some excerpts from Senator Fong's views on compulsory military service for women:

"Once women are registered, the question arises whether women must be assigned on an equal basis for all types of military service. If women are found physically qualified (under the same tests administered to determine men's qualifications) they will, in all likelihood, be required to serve in combat.

"The Majority Report chooses not to face this reality. On the one hand they want equal treatment in drafting women for compulsory military service, but then, not being willing to face the consequences of this action, they fall back on the words of Congresswoman Martha Griffiths, the primary sponsor of H.J. Res. 208, on the floor: 'The draft is equal. That is the thing that is equal. *But once you are in the Army you are put where the Army tells you where you are going to go.*' (Emphasis supplied.)

"Fortunately, these words were uttered by a woman. A man would have been accused of male chauvinism and of advocating discriminatory treatment of women.

"The Majority Report is replete with 'expectations'; including that women will not be 'assigned to combat posts, nor…required to engage in physical combat,' as is the case of the Israeli Army. They overlook the realities. Israeli women do not serve in the Armed Forces because of their demands for equal treatment regardless of sex, but because of Israel's small population, the services of each individual is indispensable to the defense of the country. Hence, different treatment of the women and the men in the Israeli Army is acceptable, even though incompatible with the concept of the Equal Rights Amendment.

"Interestingly, on the subject of the present service of men and women in the Israeli Army, the maintenance of 'separate and independent facilities' for women soldiers, is conceded, as is the fact that women soldiers perform tasks 'in the clerical, communication, electronics and nursing field.' These tasks are characterized in the Report as 'critical noncombatant tasks,'—yet, women are assigned these tasks on the basis of sex.

"Hence, under H.J. Res. 208, as reported out by the Senate Judiciary Committee, it is my firm conviction that if women pass the same tests as given men prior to assignment to duty, they must also serve on combat duty, if found qualified for such duty.

"Furthermore, the Department of Defense points out that if women could not be assigned to field duty, it might result in a disproportionate number of men serving more time in the field and on-board ship because there would be a reduced number of positions available for their reassignment to non-combat duty. That would clearly be discriminatory against men—unless all persons who serve on combat duty are released from service in a shorter period of time. This same situation applies to the Army, Navy, Marine Corps, Air Force, Merchant Marine and the Coast Guard.

"Separate units for women will, I believe, be abolished just as separate ethnic and racial units in the Armed Forces have been abolished—both men and women will serve in the same units. What privacy women will be able to be afforded, if any, is uncertain. The Department of Transportation has already published in the Federal Register its notice of proposed rule-making to amend Coast Guard regulations to allow female members of the crew to use washrooms and toilet rooms that are used by male crew members. This, I believe, is indicative of the future if women are subjected to the draft.

"For all the above set forth reasons, I am not ready or willing to support compulsory military service. If and when an all-volunteer military force comes into being, of course those women who wish to volunteer and serve in the field or on-board ships may do so. But, so long as we have a draft law, I intend to vote to exempt women from compulsory military service, and to support such modification of the Equal Rights Amendment."

Chapter 5

ERA Won't Help Women in Education
September 1973

S peakers promoting the Equal Rights Amendment often cite "education" as one area where ERA would remedy discrimination against women. This argument is false.

There is nothing ERA would do to benefit women in education. It will not give them more opportunities, more pay, or more promotions.

ERA proponents usually start off by weeping crocodile tears about discriminations against women which disappeared decades ago, such as women being denied admission to law schools, medical schools, and other graduate schools. This argument belongs in the same chip-on-the-shoulder category as crying about women not having the right to vote. ERA proponents then proceed to relate how women in education are underpaid and denied promotions, some of which is undoubtedly true. What is emphatically not true is that ERA is the remedy.

The principal reason ERA will not remedy any alleged discrimination against women in education is that Federal legislation is already more than adequate to assure women of everything they could reasonably want. Women are fully guaranteed equality in educational opportunities, admissions, and employment. This equality is spelled out in various Federal laws and enforced by the ubiquitous Federal bureaucracy.

The leading Congressional proponent of the Equal Rights Amendment, Congresswoman Martha Griffiths, put a statement in the *Congressional Record* on February 28, 1973, in which the leading activist organization promoting equality for women in education, the Women's Equity Action League (WEAL), boasted that, "When the 92nd Congress adjourned, academic women had almost all they had asked by way of legislation."

Almost? Well, there is a small remaining area which is not covered by current legislation, and which the Equal Rights Amendment would wipe out, namely, the undergraduate institutions of higher education which have been traditionally and continually single-sex. This would include seminaries and other religious academic institutions, military schools, and the few remaining colleges which have been traditionally for men only or for women only. The obsession of ERA proponents for a constitutional amendment which would eliminate the right of American citizens to operate or attend single-sex undergraduate colleges, seminaries, or military schools reveals a psychology of compulsion which is simply incompatible with the American traditions of freedom of speech, freedom of association, and freedom of education.

Present legislation also specifically provides that educational institutions may maintain separate living facilities for persons of different sexes. Such "discrimination" would also be eliminated by the Equal Rights Amendment.

61

The principal Federal laws which guarantee women equality of treatment in education are the following:

1. The Civil Rights Act of 1964, Title VII, which was extended in March 1972 to cover all educational institutions, public and private, regardless of whether or not they receive Federal aid.

2. The Education Amendments of June 1972, Title IX, which spell out the complete and specific prohibition against discrimination on the basis of sex in all Federally-assisted educational programs, from preschool through graduate school, public and private. (Nearly all educational institutions, in the country are "Federally-assisted" in some way.)

3. The Equal Pay Act of 1963 which requires equal pay for equal work.

4. Executive Order 11246 which established the Higher Education Guidelines and authorizes the Department of Labor, the Office for Civil Rights, and the Equal Employment Opportunity Commission:

a) to investigate employment practices;

b) to investigate "patterns of discrimination" as well as individual cases of discrimination;

c) to deny, terminate or cancel a Government contract in whole or in part, and to blacklist an institution from further Government contracts;

d) to require educational institutions to develop an "affirmative action plan" to recruit, employ and promote women (and other so-called minorities);

e) to require that "corrective goals" and "timetables" be established to fulfill an approved "affirmative action plan";

f) to alter or abolish anti-nepotism regulations of educational institutions;

g) to require educational institutions to compile data and information on race, sex, color, religion and national origin regardless of any conflicting state or local law, invoking the principle of Federal supremacy.

Ratification of the Equal Rights Amendment would not benefit women in education in any possible way. It would, however, gravely interfere with present educational rights which are retained by our people, and it would accelerate the meddling activism of Federal bureaucrats in every remaining aspect of our educational system.

Chapter 6
How ERA Will Hurt Divorced Women
May 1974

P revious issues of the Phyllis Schlafly Report have dealt in detail with the rights enjoyed by a wife in an ongoing marriage which will be wiped out if the Equal Rights Amendment is ever ratified. This issue discusses the rights of the divorced woman.

The divorced woman does not have the extensive rights which our laws accord to a wife. By definition, when she ceases to be a wife, she no longer enjoys the rights of a wife. However, a divorced woman does enjoy certain important rights which she will lose if the women's lib amendment is ever ratified.

Custody of Children

The most important right a divorced woman has is the presumption of custody of her children. While not usually a matter of state law, this presumption of custody is a custom so firmly engrained into our legal fabric that it has the force of law. It is a fact that, unless the mother does not want her children or there is a substantial showing that she is morally unfit to have her children, she usually is awarded custody.

The custody of her children is vitally important to a mother as she goes through the traumatic experience of a divorce. The custody of the children is what enables her to secure a reasonably fair divorce settlement from her husband, who usually has the income-producing job.

The Equal Rights Amendment would mandate the courts to make their determination on the basis of equality, or equal rights to both sexes in all matters. Equality might mean that the courts would award one child to the mother and one to the father. Or, it might mean that the courts would award custody to the father in approximately half the cases and order the mother to pay child support.

This has already happened where a local ERA has gone into effect. In a divorce case in Washington, D.C., on February 24, 1973, Superior Court Judge George W. Draper awarded the husband custody of his three children and ordered the children's mother to pay child support. He based his ruling on a little noticed change in the District of Columbia code (three years before) which mandates equality, plus what he called "the improved economic position of women generally in our society." In this case, both parents had government jobs earning about $17,000 per year.

So now the divorced woman has her job, but she has lost her three children, ages 9, 7 and 5. Any way the courts slice it, "equality" means a reduction of rights which women formerly possessed.

Child Support

The second important right now enjoyed by a divorced woman is the right to have the court compel her ex-husband to support her minor children. Either by statute, or by common law, or by case law, the father has always had the moral and legal obligation to support his minor children, regardless of whether the marriage has broken up, and regardless of whether they live with him or not. When a divorce takes place, love has usually gone out the window; but the duty to support the children remains, and this obligation is enforceable by the courts.

The Equal Rights Amendment, if ratified, would invalidate any law or court order which imposes the obligation of child support on the father because he is the father.

The states which have passed a state Equal Rights Amendment into their state constitution have given us a preview of what will happen nationally if ERA is ever ratified. Pennsylvania is one of these states. On March 26, 1974, the Pennsylvania Supreme Court handed down a decision in the case of *Conway v. Dana* which invalidated any presumption that the father, just because he is a man, has the liability for the support of his minor children. The Supreme Court listed all the previous Pennsylvania cases holding that "the primary duty of support for a minor child rests with the father." Then, the court stated that these cases "may no longer be followed" because "such a presumption is clearly a vestige of the past and incompatible with the present recognition of equality of the sexes."

From now on, the court said, the support of children will be "the equal responsibility of both father and mother."

Thus, "equality of the sexes" emphatically means that the mother must share equally in the liability to provide the financial support of her children. They call this "equal rights"—but for the divorced woman, ERA is truly the "Extra Responsibilities Amendment."

We are fortunate that Pennsylvania has given us a preview of what ERA will mean—before it is too late.

If ERA is ratified as part of the U.S. Constitution, will its effect on the obligation of fathers to support their children be retroactive? No one knows the answer to that question for sure. But we do know that the U.S. House Judiciary Committee, in its majority report on ERA (Report No. 92-359), stated:

"In some cases it would relieve the fathers of the primary responsibility for the support of even infant children, as well as the support of the mothers of such children and cast doubt on the validity of the millions of support decrees presently in existence."

Alimony

The third important right of divorced women is alimony, when ordered by the court. Alimony is certainly not a right of all divorced women; it depends on the circumstances, the length of the marriage, and other factors. But is a benefit generally given to wives, not to husbands. The dictionary defines "alimony" as "an allowance paid to a woman by her husband or former husband for her maintenance, granted by a court upon a legal separation or a divorce or while action is pending." The majority of states give alimony to wives only and not to husbands. Such a preferential benefit to women could never be tolerated under ERA.

What will happen generally to alimony under ERA is what already has happened in Georgia, where on January 24, 1974, a court declared that all alimony payments are unconstitutional in Georgia. In the case of *Murphy v. Murphy*, the court held that alimony is unconstitutional because it discriminates against husbands.

Georgia does not have a state ERA—the court merely got carried away with the new equality craze and held that alimony violates the Due Process and Equal Protection Clauses of the 5th and 14th Amendments. In a hundred years of prior litigation, no court had ever previously found that alimony was forbidden by the 5th and 14th Amendments.

That Georgia judge may be reversed on appeal; but his decision stands as a significant case of how judges often go far beyond what the law intends. This is the same kind of extrapolation of the law which the U.S. Supreme Court has been doing for the last 20 years. If the courts ever have ERA as a springboard, they may go as far afield as they have already gone with the busing and prayer decisions. Even without the Equal Rights Amendment, the courts are already ordering women admitted to men's saloons and girls admitted to Little League baseball.

The ERA proponents have been solemnly assuring us that, when confronted with a law which confers a benefit on women, the courts will extend that benefit to men rather than invalidating the benefit for women. The Georgia case proves again that this prediction is completely untrue. The Georgia court did not extend alimony to men—it simply wiped it out for women.

The respected legal publication, *United States Law Week*, commented on this decision by saying, "Women's quest for equality proves to be a boon to 'liberated' husbands."

Support of Husband?

But not getting her children, and not getting child support, and not getting alimony, is not the end of the harm which ERA will do to the divorced woman. The effect may be worse still, when a mean husband goes to court to win his full equal rights under ERA. How this can happen is illustrated by a current case now in litigation in the St. Louis, Missouri, Circuit Court: *Oakley v. Oakley*. Missouri does not have a state ERA, but its new no-fault divorce law ended the age-old requirement that the husband is always responsible to provide support for his ex-wife.

William Oakley is a male student in a freshman class at the St. Louis Municipal School of Nursing. He is suing his ex-wife for $100 a month support money for his remaining three years in nursing school, plus two years of studying the specialty he hopes to pursue, anesthesiology. He is also seeking custody of their two-year-old daughter, and an additional $100 per month in child support. Oakley's ex-wife earns about $375 per month as a clerk-typist.

It is anybody's guess who will win this case. The drafters of the new Missouri state law are expecting more and more men to start taking advantage of their new equal rights. The Oakley case is merely the first.

Effect on Senior Women

Of all classes of women, ERA is apt to hurt the senior woman the most. Consider the case of a wife in her fifties whose husband decides he wants to divorce her and marry a younger woman. This has become easier and more frequent, especially with no-fault divorce in many states.

If ERA is ratified, thereby wiping out the state laws which require a husband to support his wife, the cast-off wife will have to hunt for a job to support herself. No matter that she has made being a wife and mother her fulltime career for 20 to 30 years. No matter that she is in her fifties and unprepared to enter the competitive job market. No matter that discrimination against age deals her a double blow.

Thus, the most tragic effect of ERA can fall on the woman who has been a good wife for 20 or 30 years, and who can now be turned out to pasture with impunity. This is what equality means.

In 1973, the Virginia Legislature appointed a Task Force to study the effect which the Equal Rights Amendment would have on Virginia Law. The 97-page report was published on January 15, 1974. This report shows the adverse effect ERA would have on senior women. Present Virginia law requires children 17 or over to support their father if he is in need and is incapacitated but requires them to support their mother if she is in need, no matter what her age or capabilities. The Virginia Task Force Report clearly states that this statute "accords unequal rights" and "hence it would not meet the requirements of the Equal Rights Amendment."

Thus, if ERA is ratified, the aged and faithful mother, who has made her family her lifetime career, would have no legal right to be supported, but would be faced with having to take any job she could get if her husband and children did not voluntarily choose to support her.

Chapter 7
How ERA Will Affect Social Security
October 1974

Will the Equal Rights Amendment wipe out the right of wives to receive Social Security benefits? This is the great unanswered question that hangs over ratification of ERA as a constitutional amendment. The truthful answer is—nobody can say for sure one way or the other, because it would be up to the U.S. Supreme Court after ERA is ratified and has already gone into effect. By then, it will be too late to reject ERA if we don't like the Supreme Court decision.

Few principles are so deeply ingrained into American law as the obligation of the husband to support his wife in an ongoing marriage. This obligation is basic to the marriage contract and is recognized and fortified in an endless network of Federal and state statutes and in Federal and state case law.

One of the many manifestations of the husband's obligation is reflected in the Social Security system. A woman whose fulltime career has been as wife and mother—who has never held any paid employment outside the home (or has been employed for only a few years)—is nevertheless eligible to receive Social Security benefits based on her husband's earnings. This is one of the great preferential benefits that women receive under American laws. These preferential benefits recognize the dignity and worth of the woman who makes her career in the home.

For most of the years that Social Security has been in existence, women in paid jobs also had preferential treatment over men. Their benefits were figured on a different table from that of men—a table that gave working women larger cash benefits than received by men who had put into the system the same amount of earnings. Also, women could retire three years earlier than men.

These higher Social Security benefits were sustained by the Federal courts. (Gruenwald v. Gardner, 390 F. 2d 591 (2d Cir.), cert, denied, 393 U.S. 982, 1968.) According to Professor Paul A. Freund of the Harvard Law School, "presumably the (Equal Rights) Amendment would require a different result." (Harvard Civil Rights-Civil Liberties Law Review, March 1971, page 238.) Unfortunately, in the last couple of years, these preferential benefits for working women have been phased out under the drive for a literal equality between the sexes.

But the great preferential treatment of wives still remains intact in Social Security. Wives now collect Social Security benefits based on their husband's earnings, and this "discrimination" in favor of wives is in turn based on the legally recognized obligation of the husband to support his wife.

We know positively that the Equal Rights Amendment will make unconstitutional all the state laws of the 50 states which impose on husbands the legal duty to support their wives. This has been fully documented in many previous issues of the Phyllis

Schlafly Report. We have already seen this happen both by court decision and by statute amendment in Colorado, where a state ERA already requires a strict rule of sex equality.

Since ERA will wipe out all laws requiring a husband to support his wife while he is living, how can we expect to retain laws that require a husband to provide for his widow after he is dead? There can be no legal or logical basis for such a "discrimination." When we wipe out the principle of law that a husband must support his wife or widow in retirement, then there would be no right of a wife or widow to collect Social Security benefits based on her husband's earnings.

ERA proponents confidently claim, as Congresswoman Martha Griffiths has stated, "The Equal Rights Amendment would not permit men and women to be treated differently under Social Security." When men and women are treated the same under Social Security, logic compels us to conclude that wives who have not held paid jobs could no longer receive their preferential Social Security treatment.

When each person is treated equally, regardless of sex, women will be the clear losers. Most wives outlive their husbands, and anything that degrades the right of the wife to be provided for by her husband from his earnings is most painfully hurtful to the wife or widow at a time of life when she is most vulnerable.

If ERA is ever ratified, of course, there will be court cases. As Professor Paul Freund testified before the Judiciary Committee, "If anything about this proposed Amendment is clear, it is that it would transform every provision of law concerning women into a constitutional issue to be ultimately resolved by the Supreme Court of the United States."

Who knows what the Supreme Court will do? The U.S. Supreme Court has rendered all sorts of unpredictable decisions in the areas of crime, education, busing, security risks, pornography, abortion, and states' rights. More and more, we are finding that the attitude of the courts is, "Lady, you asked for equality; now we'll give it to you."

Senator Sam Ervin, Jr., summed up the problem very well when he told the U.S. Senate on March 22, 1972, "I believe that the Supreme Court will reach the conclusion that the ERA annuls every existing Federal and state law making any distinction between men and women, however reasonable such distinction might be in particular cases, and forever rob the Congress and the legislatures of the 50 states of the constitutional power to enact any such laws at any time in the future."

Why take a chance on losing your Social Security benefits? By the time ERA gets to the U.S. Supreme Court, it will be too late to do anything. Ask your state legislators to reject ERA now!

Chapter 8
ERA Means Abortion & Population Shrinkage
December 1974

"Legal Abortion Loses Some of Its Proponents" was a big headline in the Chicago Tribune of November 17, 1974, over an article that began, "Many advocates of legal abortion, who at first were jubilant over the Supreme Court decision legalizing abortion on demand, now think that the decision may have gone too far, according to a leading expert on fetal research."

The expert quoted in the article was Dr. Robert E. Cooke, vice chancellor for health services at the University of Wisconsin and newly-appointed head of the Federal Government's National Commission for the Protection of Human Subjects. What has changed the feelings of many original supporters of legal abortion, he said, is the several hundred fetuses born alive each year as a result of abortions. A number of these babies have survived, and a few have been adopted.

Nearly all State Legislatures have passed or are trying to pass anti-abortion legislation that will undo some if not all the damage to human life wreaked by the U.S. Supreme Court decision on abortion, or that will regulate health and safety in abortion clinics.

76

However, the facts of life-or-abortion are that, if the Equal Rights Amendment is ratified, ERA will repeal all and every kind of anti-abortion laws we now have, and prevent the enactment of any anti-abortion law in the future. If that is what you want, then the ratification of ERA will accomplish it.

ERA's Assist to Abortion

The Number One goal of the women's liberationists is, in the words of Congresswoman Bella Abzug, "to enforce the constitutional right of females to terminate pregnancies that they do not wish to continue."

There is no such "constitutional right" yet. And there won't be so long as the Equal Rights Amendment is not ratified. The current right of abortion is only a "Supreme Court right"—handed down by the U.S. Supreme Court in the case of Roe v. Wade on January 22, 1973.

The women's libbers are not satisfied with this because there is nothing in the Constitution or in any Federal law to assure that this Supreme Court right to abortion will be permanent. The Supreme Court decision was a 7-to-2 opinion, and several Justices might change their minds at any time. Or, there might be a change in the personnel of the Supreme Court. Or, Congress might pass a law removing abortion from the jurisdiction of the Supreme Court. In addition, there are dozens of State laws partially prohibiting or regulating abortion.

The women's libbers expect ERA to be the constitutional means to assure and make permanent their goal of unlimited abortion on demand. As pointed out by Professor Joseph Witherspoon, Professor of Law at the University of Texas Law School and the Texas Director of the National Right to Life Committee, "It is the hope of the abortionists that ERA will put into the Constitution what they now have only by a split Supreme Court decision."

When the women's libbers held their big rally and march to persuade Missouri to ratify ERA, their advertising read: "Saturday, Aug. 25, MARCH FOR OUR RIGHTS: to ratify the ERA in Mo., for the right to abortion in Mo. Featured speaker: Congresswoman Martha Griffiths."

The women's libbers believe that the greatest "inequality" between men and women is that women get pregnant and men do not. They want a constitutional amendment guaranteeing a strict and doctrinaire equality which will permanently protect them against anti-abortion laws.

Schools, Hospitals, and Churches

But abortion-on-demand as a private, individual right is not by any means all they want. They want to make abortion a pervasive fact of life in every aspect of our community. They want a pro-abortion public policy implemented in the following ways:

1) To require the public schools to teach abortion as a method of birth control without parental knowledge or consent (by

including this requirement in HEW regulations implementing Title IX of the Education Amendments of 1972).

2) To require the public schools to give counseling for abortion.

3) To require private and parochial schools to do both of the above, on the ground that all schools must conform to public policy in order to continue to enjoy a tax-exempt status. In August 1974, the U.S. Supreme Court accepted such a rule in regard to discrimination on the basis of race in denying tax exemption to Bob Jones University. The opinion was written by Justice Harry Blackmun, who also wrote the pro-abortion decision.

4) To require Catholic hospitals to perform abortions, on the ground that they have received grants of Federal money under the Hill-Burton Act. Nearly all Catholic hospitals have received Hill-Burton funds. Public hospitals have already been forced to perform abortions.

5) To deny tax exemption to any church that opposes abortion.

Women's Lib Weapons

These women's lib goals may sound far out, but the women's liberationists are counting on the following to achieve their goals:

1) The very language of ERA "Equality of rights under the law shall not be denied or abridged by the United States or by any State on account of sex." Since a man obviously has the right NOT

to be pregnant, the women's libbers argue that no Federal or State law against abortion would be able to deny to a woman the "equal right" NOT to be pregnant.

2) The aggressive push by the militant women's libbers, such as the National Organization for Women, whose stated goals are (a) ratification of the Equal Rights Amendment and (b) abortion. NOW welcomes lesbians as officers, but prohibits women opposed to abortion from becoming officers of NOW.

3) The high-priced legal talent available through the American Civil Liberties Union and other special interest groups to initiate and appeal lawsuits until the so-called "equal right" of abortion is permanently recognized by the courts.

4) The immense funding available to push ERA from the Rockefeller Foundation, *Playboy Magazine*, and other pro-abortion sources.

In order to try to separate ERA from the abortion issue, ERA proponents in some areas have formed a few little committees under such names as "Life and Equality." Consisting of only a handful of women, these are phony fronts designed to mislead the public, and are generally recognized as such (e.g., by the Missouri Legislators at the 1974 hearing).

In any event, these few people are irrelevant to the fact that ERA will invalidate all Congressional and State laws prohibiting or regulating abortion. Likewise, it makes no difference how many heterosexuals are promoting ERA, the fact remains that the best legal opinion is that ERA will legalize homosexual marriages and grant them the legal rights of husbands and wives.

No Arguments for ERA

Since the ERA proponents have now achieved everything they want in employment by the Equal Employment Opportunity Act of 1972, and everything they want in education by the Education Amendments of 1972 as implemented by the HEW regulations of 1974, and everything they want in credit by the passage of the Depository Institutions Amendments Act of 1974, only the permanent legalization of abortion and homosexuality could provide the motivating force for the well-financed campaign for ERA.

ERA makes no sense whatsoever in terms of any of the public statements and literature distributed in behalf of it. Every argument the proponents make can be conclusively demonstrated to be either phony, or rendered obsolete by the passage of existing legislation, or opposed by the majority of Americans.

ERA's Purpose: To Shrink Population

The "U.S. Commission on Population Growth and the American Future," established in 1970 and headed by John D. Rockefeller III, proposed a broad range of policies to stop U.S. population growth, including abortion, contraceptive services, and voluntary sterilization, through public and private financing. The Rockefeller Commission recommendations issued March 27, 1972, included the following:

"Therefore, with the admonition that abortion not be considered a primary means of fertility control, the Commission recommends that present state laws restricting abortion be liberalized along the lines of the New York State statute, such abortions to be performed on request by duly licensed physicians under conditions of medical safety.

"In carrying out this policy, the Commission recommends:

"That Federal, State and local governments make funds available to support abortion services in States with liberalized statutes.

"That abortion be specifically included in comprehensive health insurance benefits, both public and private."

Commission Pushes ERA

The Rockefeller Commission admits, however, that this will not be sufficient to control U.S. population as much as the Commission desires. So, how are women going to be induced to stop having children? The Commission states quite frankly that the Equal Rights Amendment is the means to achieving their anti-childbearing objective. Here is how the Rockefeller Commission puts it:

"In order to neutralize the legal, social, and institutional pressures that historically have encouraged childbearing, as well as to equalize opportunities generally, we should eliminate discrimination based on sex by adopting the proposed Equal Rights Amendment to the Constitution."

That makes it clear that the primary purpose of the Equal Rights Amendment, according to the Rockefeller Commission, is to shrink our population. Only secondarily, and probably only incidentally, is there any interest in any alleged equalization of opportunities. The purpose of ERA is thus to get women out of the homes so they won't be tempted to have many, or any, children. The social planners expect to accomplish this by wiping out the legal rights, the social prestige, and the institutional and economic safeguards that persuade a wife and mother to make the home her fulltime career.

A flood of magazine articles and conferences are providing the philosophical backup for the Rockefeller Commission rationale about population shrinkage via the "liberation" of women. Here are several typical examples:

An article by Lester Brown called "Alternatives to Childbearing" in the Saturday Review/World (July 27, 1974, page 47) states, "In order to reduce fertility to the levels proposed earlier, average fertility levels...will have to fall well below replacement. If a substantial share of the women in any given society seek methods of self-fulfillment other than childbearing, this fertility goal could be much more easily attained...

"Given the need to reduce fertility and birthrates, it is now imperative for every society to create employment opportunities for women sufficiently attractive to induce many of them to opt for these rather than for childbearing...We appear to be on the verge of a major restructuring of society...given both...the desire of women for a more equitable role and the pressing need to reduce fertility throughout the world. In the future, more and more women can be expected to strive for a role in society virtually indistinguishable from that of men."

Involuntary "Liberation"

An article by Jeanne Binstock called "Motherhood: An Occupation Facing Decline" in The Futurist (June 1972, page 99) states, "We are forced to face the fact that if we do not take from women their role of mother and replace it with something else, we will be throttled by the overproduction of babies. We thus face the need to demand that the ancient and honorable occupation of motherhood fall into disrepute, and that women commit themselves to other occupations. Women must be 'liberated' to enjoy the fruits of other occupations, whether they want to be or not.

"Ultimately, when women have a free choice of economic roles and their identities are no longer tied to motherhood and the traditional feminine virtues associated with it, we may be quite surprised to discover that no more women will choose to be mothers than men will choose to be engineers—and that kind of choice is what is needed if we are to solve the population problem.

"Unisex will come into fashion as a consequence of free choice. Nothing will distinguish men and women, socially and occupationally, from each other."

An article by Congresswoman Patsy T. Mink called "Women's Stake" in the New York Times (April 30, 1972, Section 12) states, "Keeping women in the home may be the major contributor to excess population growth...If we encourage policies which will permit women to choose other roles, many will leave the home and thus decide to have fewer children. We should encourage this movement of women into the work force...It is not coincidental that many of the goals of 'Women's Liberation' center on getting out of the traditional home role."

At the United Nations World Population Conference held at Bucharest in 1974, it was clearly stated in the text of the "World Population Plan of Action," immediately after expressing the hope that "the birth rate in the United States will continue to drop," that "The interrelationship of the status of women and family planning has been noted by the Assistant Secretary General of the United Nations, Helvi Sipila. Countries should make every effort to fully integrate women into all aspects of society."

During the week of November 10, 1974, a seminar entitled "Women and Population" was held in New York City designed to mesh the themes of World Population Year (1974) and International Women's Year (1975). The New York Times reported that, "despite the contrast in opinion" at the seminar, one of the conclusions was, "Fertility control will invariably fail if it is not incorporated into comprehensive, massive improvements in the education and employment of women. In other words, if a woman has nothing else from which to derive purpose, she will bear children...Population growth must be curbed. And the key to its stabilization...lies largely in global alteration of woman's lot."

The Money Connection

Abortion and ERA are tied together by a knot of money. This can be clearly seen by asking the twin questions: Who is the largest financial contributor to the pro-abortion drive? Who is the largest financial contributor to the pro-ERA drive? The answer is one and the same—Rockefeller.

The intimate relationship of the Rockefellers to population shrinkage and abortion, and their expenditure of millions of dollars for those purposes, has been extensively documented in materials easily available to the public. A good summary was given by Charles E. Rice, Professor of Law at Notre Dame Law School and a member of the National Advisory Board of the U.S. Coalition for Life, in his testimony before the Senate Committee on Rules and Administration in opposition to the nomination of Nelson A. Rockefeller for Vice President.

Professor Rice stated, "The Rockefellers' involvement in population control spans more than half a century...There are numerous examples...of substantial subsidization by the Rockefeller interests of population control centers, foundations, and other activities...

"The Rockefeller Foundation and the Rockefeller Brothers Fund have been actively involved in this population control movement, as has been the Population Council which was organized by John D. Rockefeller III in 1952. The Population Council has been particularly notable in its encouragement of liberalized abortion laws as well as governmental promotion of sterilization and contraception...

"Nelson Rockefeller is perhaps the leading proponent of permissive abortion in the United States. He strongly supported the 1970 enactment in New York of what was then the most permissive abortion law in the United States. Then when the Legislature repealed that law in 1972, Governor Rockefeller vetoed that repeal. He is a strong supporter of the 1973 abortion decisions of the United States Supreme Court...

"He is more than any other person, the incarnate symbol of the anti-life movement in the United States..."

And ERA, Also

Likewise, the Rockefeller Foundation is the largest financial contributor to the pro-ERA propaganda push. On March 1, 1974, the Rockefeller Foundation granted $288,000 to the California Commission on the Status of Women. In announcing the grant, Commission Chairwoman Anita Miller said that it will be used for "a 'mass education process' to inform Americans of the meaning and consequences of the ERA."

Can it be inferred that this "mass education process" might tell the adverse effects of ERA? Absolutely not! Ms. Miller boasted that her Commission had already pushed successfully for ratification of ERA by the California Legislature, and she gleefully predicted that ERA will be "the single most significant event of this century...It will bring about a dimension of change greater than ever before."

Indeed it will—if it is ratified. And Ms. Miller has $288,000 of Rockefeller Foundation money to bring about this change.

Another very wealthy and influential anti-family, anti-children, and pro-ERA force is *Playboy Magazine*. It was revealed at the Illinois Legislative hearing in 1974 that substantial cash contributions and the use of the *Playboy* postage meter for mailings all over the State have been supplied by *Playboy Magazine* to the pro-ERA headquarters in Chicago.

Rockefeller and *Playboy* money will soon be supplemented by Federal funds to push the "liberation" of women from the home to join the work force and thus opt out of the role of mother. President Ford, in signing the Elementary and Secondary Education Act Amendments of 1974, gave HEW the authority to spend millions of dollars annually for the purpose of "desexing" textbooks. That is lib jargon for removing the stories and pictures portraying women in the home and replacing them with women in "active" roles (such as construction work, etc.). This is the way our young girls will be cheated out of knowing about the joys and fulfillment of making a career as wife and mother. Our young women will thus be "liberated" from the home "whether they want to be or not."

If this is not the future you want for your daughters, you had better act fast to defeat ERA.

Chapter 9
ERA Will Doom Fraternities & Sororities
January 1975

I f the Equal Rights Amendment is ever ratified, it will prohibit fraternities and sororities from functioning on college campuses. This is the shocking new information that has come to light and stirred up a hornet's nest in the educational world.

In June 1972, Congress passed the Education Amendments which included this seemingly simple language in Title IX: "No person in the United States shall, on the basis of sex, be excluded from participation in, be denied the benefits of, or be subjected to discrimination under any educational program or activity receiving Federal financial assistance."

Two years later, on June 18, 1974, the Department of Health, Education and Welfare issued 80 pages of proposed regulations "to effectuate Title IX of the Education Amendments of 1972." In regard to fraternities, sororities, and other campus organizations, these HEW regulations stated, "A recipient (any college, university, or state receiving any Federal assistance) may not, in connection with its educational program or activity, support or assist any organization, agency or person which discriminates on the basis of sex."

The HEW regulations then give this specific example of the application of this rule, "A recipient educational institution would be prohibited from providing financial support for an all-female hiking club, an all-male language club, or a single-sex honorary society. However, an organization whose membership was restricted to members of one sex could adhere to its restrictive policies, and operate on the campus of a recipient university, if it received no support or housing from the university and did not operate in connection with the university's education program or activity."

Meanwhile, in certain areas HEW proceeded with highly aggressive action. HEW began monitoring all fraternities and sororities at Southern Methodist University, requiring statistical reports that include the sex and ethnic identity of each rushee from the sign-up stage through initiation. HEW is also using its lawsuit against Delta Sigma Pi to establish its jurisdiction over fraternities and sororities.

Wow! As soon as fraternities and sororities began to feel the impact of these HEW regulations, they went into action and issued memorandum alerts to their membership. Here are some excerpts from one letter issued by the international president of one sorority.

Sorority Alert

"The proposed regulation…reaches into the rights of organizations in the schools. A recipient educational institution would be prohibited from providing financial support for a single-sex honorary society, such as Mortar Board or Alpha Lambda Delta, or a single-sex organization such as the Association of Women Students or Campus Panhellenic.

"And, most vital to sororities is the provision that institutions may permit single-sex organizations, such as fraternities and sororities, to operate on campus only if they 'receive no support or housing from the university and did not operate in connection with the university's education program or activity.'

"Officials of HEW do not define 'support.' Does this mean fraternities may not use meeting rooms in a college building? What about chapters which have built houses on land leased from the schools, or who have houses or lodges which are owned by the schools? Does "support' mean recognition? And what is an education 'activity'?...

"The ramifications are threatening...All of us could be in litigation for years over housing and special services. What happens to Panhellenic Houses and sorority suites in dormitories? How much does Panhellenic 'operate in connection with the university's education programs or activity,' and how is this defined? Does this mean that faculty members cannot be advisors to sororities as part of their academic duties?...

"There is potential demise of such organizations as Mortar Board and other fine groups concerned with the status of women...The law was not intended to encompass such a wide range. It appears that the guidelines (or rules) published for implementation of Title IX have gone beyond reason."

As a result of this and similar alerts sent out by fraternities and sororities, it is reported that some 9,000 letters descended on the

HEW Department. Senators and Congressmen began feeling the heat.

There were many other aspects of the 1974 HEW regulations that drew fire from other groups, such as the unreasonable HEW regulations requiring that all physical education classes and programs be sex-integrated. Others were disturbed because of the application of HEW sex-discrimination regulations to Boy and Girl Scouts, Campfire Girls, YMCAs and YWCAs.

The sponsors of the Education Amendments of 1972, including Senator Birch Bayh and Congresswoman Edith Green, raised their hands in astonishment and said they didn't mean all this! Congresswoman Green said that Title IX "wasn't designed to do any of this nonsense."

It is hard to see how they could be surprised. What HEW did was wholly predictable. The HEW bureaucrats utilized the broad scope of the law to proceed with aggressive and specific implementation, following the same pattern of their use of the Civil Rights Act of 1964 to require forced busing.

HEW Secretary Caspar Weinberger indicated sympathy with the complaints of fraternities and sororities but stated that Congress would have to pass specific legislation before he would change the regulations. Obviously, he feels that the Education Amendments of 1972 require and authorize the regulations that HEW issued, including their application to fraternities and sororities.

Congresswoman Edith Green quickly persuaded a Senate-House conference committee to approve an amendment to the HEW appropriations bill ordering HEW not to apply sex-discrimination rules to college and high school fraternities and sororities, Boy and Girl Scouts, Campfire Girls, YMCAs and YWCAs, and Boys Club and Girls Club, and prohibiting the use of Federal funds "to enforce the integration of physical education classes by sex."

Not Far Enough!

While Congressmen, fraternities and sororities have been valiantly trying to bring some sanity into this picture, the women's lib groups are complaining that the HEW regulations did not go far enough! In many states, the state committees set up to study the HEW regulations are dominated by members of the National Organization for Women, who are stridently demanding more and faster sex-integration in every aspect of the entire educational process. Four women's groups have filed suit against the Government demanding more aggressive enforcement of the laws and regulations against sex discrimination.

The Chronicle of Higher Education quoted one spokeswoman for a women's group opposing the exemption of fraternities and sororities from sex discrimination regulations. She said, "Fraternities and sororities are places where the old-boy network operates and contacts are made. To exempt them is to exclude women from future job opportunities."

It is probable that Congress will soon pass specific amendments to the Education Amendments of 1972 which make sure that fraternities and sororities are exempted from the laws and HEW regulations. Such exemptions are wholly reasonable and desirable, and certainly the majority of Americans have no wish to wipe out the single-sex nature of fraternities and sororities. These organizations are entitled to their freedom of association, and they serve a valuable role in the educational world.

What ERA Will Do

But the inescapable, irrefutable fact is that, if the Equal Rights Amendment is ever ratified, any exemption passed by Congress would immediately become unconstitutional and invalid. All the effort expended by the fraternities and sororities to persuade Congress to pass legislation exempting them will be to no avail—if ERA is ever ratified. As every informed person knows, Congress can amend any law by the single expedient of passing an amendment by majority vote. But Congress cannot amend or change a constitutional amendment once it has been sent out to the states for ratification. The only way a constitutional amendment can be changed or modified, or exemptions added to it, is by the long, agonizing process of passing another constitutional amendment. We have done that only once in the nearly 200 years of our Republic (when we passed the repeal of Prohibition).

The furor about the fraternities and sororities proves several important lessons:

1) An absolute rule against discrimination on the basis of sex has consequences that are ridiculous, unreasonable, and unwanted by the majority of Americans.

2) A law whose language sounds desirable or innocuous can easily become a fearful weapon of regulation and control in the hands of the bureaucrats who implement it and the courts that enforce it.

When the Equal Rights Amendment was being passed by Congress and during its early months of ratification by the states, the proponents solemnly assured everyone that it referred only to Federal and State laws, to employment and higher educational opportunities for women, and would not interfere in the "private sector." This is probably why such essentially private organizations as fraternities and sororities did not recognize the threat to their very existence in the disarming language of ERA.

It is now clear that the ERA proponents, armed with the immense power of the Federal bureaucracy and the Federal courts, are going to use every legal technicality and loophole to achieve full sex-integration at every level, public and private, whether it is desired or not by the public or by the persons directly involved. Thus, the sex-integration pushers have been waging war in the courts on Little League baseball, the Jaycees, Kiwanis and other men's service clubs, and men's bars such as the famous Mory's at Yale. There is no question but that ERA will give these sex-integration pushers the weapon they need to destroy fraternities and sororities as they are now constituted.

The abolition of the single-sex status of fraternities, sororities and other campus organizations is only one of the unreasonable effects on education that would be caused by ratification of the Equal Rights Amendment. ERA will also require all single-sex colleges to go coed if they receive any Federal aid or grants whatsoever. This would include Smith, Wellesley, Mount Holyoke, Bryn Mawr, and Stephens Colleges. ERA will make all the military academies go coed and will apply reverse discrimination to make them 50 percent women.

Furthermore, a recent Internal Revenue ruling and Supreme Court decision indicate that, on the rule that mere tax-exempt status in itself constitutes the conferring of a Federal benefit, ERA would probably wipe out our right to have single-sex educational institutions at any level, and thereby eliminate single-sex grade schools, high schools and colleges holding tax-exempt status, even though they receive no Federal aid at all. This would be the unreasoning and undesirable application of a constitutional rule for sex equality.

If you support legislation to exempt fraternities and sororities, Boy and Girl Scouts, Campfire Girls, YMCAs and YWCAs, and physical education classes from Title IX of the Education Amendments of 1972, then you must work rapidly to defeat ratification of the Equal Rights Amendment, or it will be too late. If you are in a state that has not yet ratified, ask your state legislators to Vote NO. If you are in a state that has already ratified, ask your state legislators to rescind their previous ratification in the light of the new evidence uncovered by the HEW regulations.

Chapter 10
How ERA Will Affect Churches & Private Schools
March 1975

Everyone knows that schools, colleges, and other institutions that receive Federal aid are subject to Federal control and regulations. The long hand of Federal control, however, has now been extended by administrative ruling and by U.S. Supreme Court decision into the vast area of private schools, colleges and institutions that hold tax-exempt status, even though they do not receive any Federal aid whatsoever. If their ability to seek and obtain tax-deductible contributions is taken away, most private schools, colleges, and institutions will be forced to close their doors.

Federal statutes authorize tax exemption for institutions and organizations operated exclusively for religious, educational, or charitable purposes. The Federal statute on tax exemption does not mention "discrimination."

In 1971, however, the Internal Revenue Service issued the following ruling, "A private school that does not have a racially nondiscriminatory policy as to students does not qualify for exemptions." (Rev. Rul. 71-447, 1971-2 CB 230.)

Bob Jones University in South Carolina is a private, religious college that does not receive any Federal aid whatsoever. In

1972 the Internal Revenue Service withdrew its tax-exempt status on the ground that the University discriminates in its admissions policy on the basis of race. Bob Jones University challenged this ruling in the Federal courts.

U.S. Supreme Court Decision

On May 15, 1974, the U.S. Supreme Court handed down a decision in the case of Bob Jones University v. William E. Simon, Secretary of the Treasury. This decision said that Bob Jones University could not enjoin the Internal Revenue Service from carrying out its "newly announced policy of denying tax-exempt status for private schools with racially discriminatory admissions policies" and from revoking "a ruling letter declaring that petitioner [Bob Jones University] qualified for tax-exempt status."

Anyone involved in religious, educational or charitable work knows the importance of tax-exempt status under Section 501(c)(3) of the Internal Revenue Code, and of being able to solicit tax-deductible contributions under Section 170(c)(2). When an institution or organization receives tax-exempt status from the Internal Revenue Service, it receives a "ruling letter" and is listed on the "Cumulative List." The U.S. Supreme Court opinion in the Bob Jones University case recognized the importance of this status, saying, "Appearance on the Cumulative List is a prerequisite to successful fund-raising for most charitable organizations. Many contributors simply will not make donations to an organization that does not appear on the Cumulative List."

Strict Rule Against Sex Discrimination

While most Americans (including the writer of this article) do not agree with the policies of Bob Jones University, it is important for all Americans to understand clearly what changes would take place in our society if the Internal Revenue Service and the U.S. Supreme Court are constitutionally compelled to apply the same strict rule against sex discrimination that they now apply to race discrimination.

The Equal Rights Amendment is a proposed constitutional amendment which would impose a strict bar on discrimination on the basis of sex, and impose the obligation on the Federal Government to make sure that sex discrimination is eliminated from every facet of our life touched by the government. ERA reads clearly, positively, and absolutely:

"Section 1: Equality of rights under the law shall not be denied or abridged by the United States or by any State on account of sex.

"Section 2: The Congress shall have the power to enforce, by appropriate legislation, the provisions of this article."

The Equal Rights Amendment will require the same absolute ban on sex discrimination that is now required against race discrimination. If the Internal Revenue Service and the U.S. Supreme Court apply the same ruling on sex that they did in the Bob Jones University case, the implications for our private schools, colleges and churches are tremendously far-reaching.

Single-Sex Schools and Colleges

Ratification of ERA would then mean that every single-sex private and religious-based school and college would be confronted with the choice of (1) abandoning its single-sex status or (2) losing its tax-exempt status. A single-sex school or college, by definition, discriminates on the basis of sex; that is, girls are barred from admission to boys' schools, and boys are barred from admission to girls' schools.

At the Missouri Senate Committee hearing on ERA on January 28, 1975, a Senator asked the lawyer for the ERA proponents if ERA would deprive single-sex private and religious schools and colleges of their tax-exemption. She readily agreed that ERA would require this, and added that the proponents want this because they object to tax-exemption for any school of college that discriminates on the basis of sex in its admissions policy.

The Senator then carried this one step further and questioned her about the tax-exempt status of churches that discriminate on the basis of sex. She would not confirm or deny whether ERA would empower the Internal Revenue Service to withdraw tax exemption from churches that discriminate on the basis of sex.

However, the logic of assuming that the Internal Revenue Service and the U.S. Supreme Court would, indeed, do this, is compelling.

Churches Ordaining Women

This question opens up a whole new area of undesirable and unwanted effects of ERA. Some churches today are ordaining women as ministers, and that is their right to do so. Other churches and synagogues do not ordain women as ministers, priests, rabbis, or bishops, and it should be their right not to do so without losing their tax-exemption. It is part of their religious faith that God has assigned a different role in this life to men and to women, and that these different roles are basic both to the ministerial mission and to the family unit.

The women's lib movement calls this "discrimination" and "stereotyping," and is making a determined drive against churches that allegedly discriminate on the basis of sex. The National Organization for Women, in its official booklet called Revolution: Tomorrow is NOW, makes the following demands: (1) that churches and seminaries immediately stop their "sexist" doctrines that assign a different role to men and women; (2) that seminaries recruit, enroll, financially aid, employ, and promote women theologians and theological students on an equal basis with men; (3) that Federal statutes be amended and enforced to deprive churches of their right to discriminate on the basis of sex; and, (4) that tax-exemption be withdrawn from any church actively opposed to abortion.

ERA or Freedom of Religion

It is unrealistic to assume that the constitutional guarantees of freedom of religion and separation of church and state will prevent the courts from interfering to abolish sex discrimination. While the courts have been reluctant to take jurisdiction over the internal affairs of a church or religious organization, they will step in when civil rights are involved. The courts have stepped in to protect the civil rights of children when Jehovah's Witnesses denied blood transfusions to their children for religious reasons. The courts have stepped in to order compulsory school attendance even though this violated the religious convictions of the Mennonites.

Bob Jones University tried to assert its First Amendment right to freedom of religion and argue that it is a religious college, and that the tenets of its religious faith require a difference in admissions policies between the races. The Internal Revenue Service and the U.S. Supreme Court rejected this argument (because Federal tax-exemption was involved) and forced freedom of religion to give way to Federal rules against race discrimination.

There is every reason to assume that, if ERA be comes the most recent constitutional amendment, the Internal Revenue Service and the U.S. Supreme Court will rule likewise on sex and allow our constitutional right to freedom of religion to be limited by the new rule requiring the Federal Government to use its power to abolish all difference of treatment between the sexes in every aspect of our lives touched by Federal and state laws—including tax-exemption under the Internal Revenue Code, Section 501(c)(3) and Section 170(c)(2).

102

The women's liberationists have access to an impressive roster of high-priced legal talent to fight their causes through the courts. The Equal Rights Amendment—with its total bar on sex discrimination—will give them the constitutional basis to achieve their objectives in forcing churches and synagogues to ordain women, and to admit them to total equality and sameness of treatment in churches, seminaries, and religious schools and organizations, or forfeit their tax-exempt status.

NBC Portrays the ERA Society

We are indebted to NBC for providing viewers with a three-hour prime-time television network presentation of the type of society that the Equal Rights Amendment will bring to America. On January 9, 1975, NBC telecast an elaborate production called "Of Women and Men" with Barbara Walters and Tom Snyder as co-anchorpersons. It was expensively advertised with full-page ads in major cities across the country. If you missed it, or turned it off from boredom or disgust, that is a pity because it was a thorough TV portrayal of the lifestyle, the morals, the religion, and the male-female relationships so stridently promoted by the advocates of ERA, women's lib, and sex liberation.

"Of Women and Men" can best be summed up as a total assault on marriage. The production was anti-marriage, anti-monogamy, anti-morality, and anti-Bible. Sex without marriage was presented as the accepted way of life at all ages, from the high school students whose weekend dates are in closed vans outfitted with wall-to-wall carpeting and overhead mirrors, to the man and woman in their seventies who frankly described sharing an apartment and enjoying sex without benefit of marriage. In between was 25-year old Erica who enthusiastically discussed how she enjoys sex with a variety of single and married men, especially group sex, and is considering homosexuality.

"Of Women and Men" included a blasphemous rewrite of the story of Adam and Eve. According to the NBC fable, God created Adam, Eve and Lilith, a militant woman's libber who intimidated even God Himself. The bond between Adam and Eve is replaced by the sisterhood of Eve and Lilith. How the human race survived is not made clear.

In all the three hours, there was not a single voice for monogamous, lifetime marriage as a satisfactory male-female relationship, for the family as the basic unit of our society, for motherhood as a fulfilling role for women, or for the Ten Commandments as a rule of conduct that binds our society together. The 100 interviews did not include a single example of a happy or stable marriage. The message given loud and clear by co-anchorpersons Walters and Synder was that a world of sex-without-marriage and "serial" marriages is coming fast and should be cheerfully welcomed. Snyder solemnly stated that marriage will no longer be for a lifetime but short-term or "serial" that is, "a series of relationships." Walters assured us that women will not be "drones" any more, thus mouthing the basic women's lib doctrine that the role of wife and mother is menial and degrading, and that the home is a prison from which women must be liberated.

"Of Women and Men" was a thorough and professional presentation of women's lib dogma, attitudes, lifestyles, values, and demands, given with unabashed approval by Walters and Synder. It portrayed the women's lib demands on schools, school textbooks, family relationships, religious literature, television programming, sexual mores, the Constitution, government programs, politics, and athletics. (The program showed a pitiful little girl boxing with a boy in a regular boxing ring, and a woman "liberated" to break her nose playing ice hockey with men.) The show even featured an interview with the godmother of women's lib, Betty Friedan, boasting that "it's revolution and it's marvelous." Not one critic of any of the women's lib proposals was given a moment on the show.

Chapter 11
How ERA Will Affect Athletics
April 1975

T he difference between rational behavior under existing law, and the irrational nonsense which will be required if the Equal Rights Amendment is ever ratified, is made crystal clear by two rulings about athletics made in March 1975.

Pennsylvania Football/Wrestling Case

Pennsylvania is one of the handful of states that have enacted a state Equal Rights Amendment, so ERA is already operative there. On March 19, 1975, the Commonwealth Court of Pennsylvania decided that girls must be permitted to practice and compete with boys in all high school athletics, including football and wrestling. In a 5-to-l decision, the Court ruled that a Pennsylvania Interscholastic Athletic Association bylaw prohibiting coeducational competition violates the Equal Rights Amendment to the Pennsylvania Constitution.

The lawyers who brought this case did not request that the Court order girls admitted to football and wrestling, but only asked an end to sex discrimination in other high school sports. The Court, however, saw no difference between football/wrestling and other sports, holding that the mandate of ERA is absolute and must apply to all sports.

The Pennsylvania Court decision is the logical result of the strict ban on sex differences required by the language of the Equal Rights Amendment. This case is a good example of the nonsense that results when we are constitutionally required to treat men and women exactly equally in absolutely everything that is touched by Federal or state law, administrative regulation, or public funding.

If the Federal Equal Rights Amendment is ratified by 38 states, we will be required to extend this sort of mischief to every school and college in the country, without exceptions, qualifications, or reasonable differences that reasonable men and women want.

New HEW Regulations on Sports

On March 29, 1975, newspapers published the new, revised regulations issued by the Department of Health, Education and Welfare to implement Title IX of the Education Amendments of 1972. The 1972 law is a strict ban on sex discrimination in all schools and colleges that receive any Federal aid or assistance whatsoever, and the original HEW regulations issued in June 1974 stirred up a storm of protest because they went too far in requiring everything to be coed, sex neutral, and gender-free. The revised 1975 regulations have now been submitted to President Ford for his approval before they go into effect.

While adhering to the general rule against sex discrimination in school and college athletics, the revised HEW regulations make the following specific exemptions:

1. In contact sports, women may not try out for men's teams even if no women's team in that sport is available. Contact sports are defined as boxing, wrestling, football, basketball, ice hockey, and rugby.

2. In non-contact sports, women may try out for men's teams if no women's team is available.

3. Physical education classes must be sex-integrated, but they may be sex-segregated for contact sports or when sex education is given.

The National Collegiate Athletic Association and others have contended that athletics should be exempted from Federal sex-discrimination rules because sports programs receive little or no direct Federal aid. The new HEW regulations, however, take the position that, if the school or college receives Federal aid for any program or activity, it is irrelevant whether the athletic program itself receives Federal aid. The HEW regulations state that athletics "constitute an integral part of the educational process of schools and colleges and, as such, are fully subject to the requirements."

Reasonable people may differ on the precise details of these regulations. If they are found to be unworkable, they can be changed by subsequent HEW regulations. If HEW proves to be obstinate, the regulations can then be changed by a Congressional amendment to the Education Amendments of 1972, which is the legislative authority for the HEW regulations.

The Nonsense of ERA

Thus, under the new HEW regulations, high schools and colleges may maintain separate teams for men and women—and women may join men's sports only in non-contact sports and only if no women's team is available. However, under ERA, it becomes unconstitutional to have separate men's or women's athletic squads in any sport, and all athletic practice must be sex-integrated, even in football and wrestling. ERA will revolutionize school and college athletics.

Women Lose Under Enforced Equality

If there is anyone who should oppose the Equal Rights Amendment, it is women athletes. If the Constitution requires and the courts rule that women must be admitted to men's sports, then it must follow as the night the day that men must be admitted to women's sports. ERA is a two-edged sword. In fact, a spokesman for the Pennsylvania Justice Department admitted this in commenting on a court decision, stating boys would have to be permitted to try out for girl's teams and vice versa.

What this means is that, at the high school and college levels, the boys who get cut from the varsity teams can switch over and compete on the girls' teams. In many sports, this will take away the facilities and the funding that are starting to open up for women in school and college-athletics.

If the same nonsensical sex equality is enforced in professional sports, this would mean that men can enter the women's tournaments and win most of the money. The large money prizes in these tournaments will enable publicity-seeking men to hire lawyers to litigate under ERA. Bobby Riggs has already publicly stated, "I think that men 55 years and over should be allowed to play women's tournaments—like the Virginia Slims. Everybody ought to know there's no sex after 55 anyway."

Whether or not the courts would extend the nonsense of ERA to professional sports, ERA absolutely must apply to all high school and college athletics. A good example of what will become the national rule in all schools and colleges, if ERA is ratified, is shown by the case of the Illinois high school bowling tournament.

Bowling Tournament in Illinois

An Illinois circuit court last year decreed that, when a school or college provides no participation for one sex in any non-contact, non-collision sport, members of that sex have the right to compete with the other sex.

In the Dixon (Illinois) High School, bowling is a non-contact sport provided for girls, but not for boys. So the boys decided they would take advantage of the new Illinois circuit court ruling, and compete for places on the girls' bowling team. Boys won four out of the five places on the Dixon High School team.

At the I.H.S.A.'s girls' state championship bowling tournament held in Peoria, Illinois, in February 1975, in front of the

110

icy glares of female rivals, their coaches and parents, the Dixon boys walked off with the title. Dixon's score of 9,749 for the two days of competition was 229 pins ahead of the runner-up team, whose coach said sadly afterwards, "We were getting tired in the finals. It's hard to bowl six games that fast under this kind of pressure—bowling against boys."

Everyone was angry about the farce. The sympathy of the crowd was certainly not with the winners. Here is a sampling of press comments:

"Boys have taken over and virtually destroyed a girls' tournament."

"What an evil joke it was to pit two fine Chicago girls' bowling teams against the boys."

"What happened in Peoria set sports in Illinois high schools back 10 years."

The Physical Difference

It is a cardinal dogma of the women's liberation movement that men and women differ only in sex organs, and that all other differences, even physical differences are due only to cultural training and societal restraints. Anyone who has fallen for this particular bit of mythology should look at the difference between men and women in the Olympic Games competitions.

Men have a tremendous advantage in all sports demanding muscle-power, speed, or endurance. In track and field, for example, individual male records surpass women's by about 10 to 18 percent.

The differential in field events is about 20 percent. Variations in swimming run about 10 percent and even higher in events such as back stroke, breast stroke, and butterfly, which place a premium on muscular output.

There are, of course, some women athletes who can out-perform the average man; but few, if any, can compete with men of similar talent and experience. In sports that do not favor muscularity and size, such as shooting and equestrian sports, women compete against men in the Olympic events. In some sports that depend on beauty and grace, such as figure skating, the women are superior and can command more money than the men.

None of this, however, in any way disputes the tremendous physical gulf in athletics that exists between women and men in most sports. Even in a completely non-contact sport, such as golf, the women are washed out of the game if they are not given the special advantage of playing from the shorter ladies' tees.

Whether you are concerned about women's athletics, or men's athletics, or simply the rationality of our educational system and its athletic program, you should act immediately to defeat the Equal Rights Amendment while there is still time to do so. Write or call your State Senators and Representatives and ask them to vote NO on ERA

Chapter 12
The Hypocrisy of ERA Proponents
July 1975

Many people are puzzled by the way 16 state legislatures rejected the Equal Rights Amendment during 1975 in spite of the fact that ERA appears to be supported by about 95 percent of the press and a long list of organizations. The explanation of this mystery lies in the great difference between what the ERA proponents say at the hearings held by the state legislatures—and what they say when they speak in the press and before women's groups. The ERA proponents tell one line to relatively uninformed audiences, but quite another line when they are subject to cross-examination by lawyer legislators at the hearings. Let us consider some of the areas where ERA proponents are betrayed by their own hypocrisy.

The Draft and Military Service

When speaking before uninformed women's groups, ERA proponents usually handle this subject with one or more of these arguments, "Oh, you don't think Congress will really draft women, do you!" Or, "All women will not be drafted." Or, "Don't worry, mothers will always be exempted just as fathers have been." Or, "If women are drafted, we won't have any more wars."

When the ERA proponents come before state legislative hearings, of course they cannot make such sleazy arguments that would be an insult to the intelligence of any legislator, lawyer, or other informed person.

Yes, Congress will really draft women if ERA is ratified because the U.S. Constitution is "the supreme law of the land," and Congress must obey it. ERA will forbid Congress, or any other federal or state law or body, to make any difference of treatment based on sex.

Nobody ever said that "all" women will be drafted. But girls of the proper age and in good physical condition will be drafted and sent into combat exactly like the men.

The argument that mothers will be exempted as fathers have always been exempted is wholly dishonest when made by any ERA proponent old enough to remember World War II, when fathers up to age 35 were drafted and sent into the fiercest kind of combat. Under ERA, any time fathers are drafted, mothers must be treated exactly the same.

The argument that drafting women will keep us out of war can only be made by those who are ignorant of history. The Arabs were not deterred from attacking Israel by the knowledge that Israeli women are drafted. And women can even start wars, as Mrs. Indira Gandhi proved when she ordered India's attack on Pakistan.

ERA proponents know they cannot get by before state legislators with such foolish arguments, because the one thing that is indisputable about ERA is that it will require federal law and military regulations to give women and men exactly the same treatment. So the ERA proponents adopt an entirely different line. They say, "We want women drafted, and we want them placed in combat; and we don't think women can achieve their full rights in our society until they are treated absolutely equally with men in every job in the military."

At the Virginia hearing, one of the legislators asked a pro-ERA witness, "If we did draft women, don't you think we could assign the women to the safe, noncombat jobs, and leave the actual fighting up to the men?" She replied: "Oh no, because that would discriminate against women and deprive us of our equal opportunity to win a Congressional Medal of Honor!" Unfortunately, most Medal of Honor winners are dead; and the overwhelming majority of American women do not think we were mistreated because we did not have an equal obligation to fight in jungle warfare in Vietnam, and become POWs and MIAs.

The ERA proponents are themselves always either over draft age, or they have no daughters, or they are too young to know what war is all about, or they concede that they personally will be conscientious objectors. They have invariably already exercised their freedom of choice to avoid military service, but they are willing to inflict involuntary military duty on all 18-year-old girls in the future.

Alan Alda, the star of the television program "M*A*S*H" whom the ERA proponents imported to Illinois to star as their lead witness at the Senate hearing, expressed himself quite willing for everyone else's daughter to be drafted; but when asked if his three daughters would be conscientious objectors, he replied, "I hope so."

Naturally, when the ERA proponents come into the hearings and tell enthusiastically about how they want ERA so women can be drafted and sent into military combat just like men, the average legislator sits there and thinks, "That surely isn't what the women in my district want." And of course it is not what women want. It is absolutely ridiculous to force all women to conform to the demands of the militant women radicals who themselves have not the slightest intention of ever serving in the military.

Employment

When speaking before women's groups and in the press, ERA proponents continue falsely to equate ERA with "equal pay for equal work" and falsely to imply that ERA will give women advantages in the field of employment that they do not now have. These claims are untrue for two reasons: (1) ERA does not even apply to private industry—it applies only to federal and state law; and (2) there is no way that ERA can extend the effect of the Equal Employment Opportunity Act of 1972. This law is completely extensive; it applies to hiring, pay, and promotion, and establishes the enforcement agency called the Equal Employment Opportunity Commission (EEOC).

Under this Commission, women have won multimillion-dollar settlements against the largest companies in the country. When they won a $38 million settlement against AT&T, women got back pay for not having been paid as much as they should have been, back pay for not having been promoted as they should have been, and even back pay for jobs that they did not apply for because they thought they would not get them! What more could any woman want by way of federal legislation to enforce equal employment opportunity?

In any event, ERA will add no new employment rights whatsoever, and it is deceitful for ERA proponents to claim or imply that it will. When ERA proponents make this argument before uninformed audiences, they are merely pandering to the natural assumption of most working women and men that they are underpaid.

When the proponents come into the state legislative hearings, where they are subject to cross-examination, it is interesting that they never claim that ERA will do anything for women in the field of employment. They know there is no substance to this argument, and they do not dare to make it. They readily concede under questioning that ERA will not help women in the field of employment.

When I debated the leading Congressional proponent of ERA, Congresswoman Martha Griffiths, I made the statement that, "ERA will do absolutely nothing for women in the field of employment." She replied, "I never claimed it would." Her concession blows the whole case of the ERA proponents in regard to jobs.

One point should be watched for in connection with ERA and employment. ERA lawyers at several hearings have tried to allege that ERA will give "equal pay for equal work" to federal, state, county, and municipal employees because they are not covered by the Equal Employment Opportunity Act of 1972. This myth was apparently fabricated by someone in the pro-ERA camp, and then circulated for use by speakers who did not do their homework on the subject. In any event, the claim is wholly untrue, as the Equal Employment Opportunity Act of 1972 specifically does cover federal, state, county, and municipal employees.

It can be stated categorically that ERA will not give women equal pay for equal work, or any new rights, choices, or opportunities that they do not now have.

Family Support

When ERA proponents speak before women's groups or in the press, they try to deny that ERA will invalidate the state laws that require a husband to support his wife and children and provide them with a home. When they come before the state legislative hearings, however, they are forced to admit under cross-examination that ERA will require the financial obligation of family support to be equal between husband and wife. This is the crux of the problem. Since there is no way yet known to make the bearing of children equal between the sexes, it is a grave injustice to the wife to make her equally financially obligated for family support.

The ERA proponents have tipped their hand by the texts of specific bills on family support that they have introduced into various state legislatures. For example, the ERA leader in the Texas

118

legislature, Representative Sarah Weddington, introduced a bill to change the family support law by the addition of a phrase to ensure complete equality. The present Texas law reads, "The husband has the duty to support the wife and the wife has the duty to support the husband when he is unable to support himself." The obligation is thus not equal. In the normal course of events, the husband has the duty to support his wife. The wife has an obligation only if the husband, for some reason, is unable to support himself (illness, incapacity, unemployment, etc.) That is a good statement of the marriage obligation. Mrs. Weddington's bill, however, would amend this law so that it would read, "The husband has the duty to support the wife when she is unable to support herself and the wife has the duty to support the husband when he is unable to support himself."

When is a wife "unable" to support herself? Only the first week after she has a baby? Or only for 56 days afterwards, as women are given in China? Or only for a few months afterwards, as women get in European Communist countries?

Under the Weddington bill, as under ERA, the wife will lose her present legal right to be supported and her right to be a fulltime wife and mother in the home, and she would be reduced to proving that "she is unable to support herself." It is hard to see how there could be a more devastating effect on the family structure and on the present legal rights of the wife. This is why Senator Sam Ervin called ERA "the most destructive piece of legislation to ever pass Congress."

This Texas bill is not unique. In Illinois the ERA sponsor, Representative Eugenia Chapman, introduced a similar amendment to change the family support law. The Illinois law now reads, "A husband is liable for the support of his wife, and a wife for the support of her husband if he is in need of such support and is, or is likely to become, a public charge." Mrs. Chapman's amendment would change the law to make the husband and wife responsible for each other's support "if either is in need of such support and is, or is likely to become, a public charge." This clearly reduces the wife's customary and primary right to financial support down to the level where she has a legal right to support only if she is "in need" or about to go on welfare.

Sometimes the ERA proponents handle the "equality" requirement for family support by replacing the "sexist" terms (man, woman, male, female, husband, wife) with the sex-neutral terms (person, spouse). Thus, after the Colorado family support law was voided by the Colorado courts under the new Colorado state equal rights amendment, the legislature changed the Colorado support law to read "person" shall support "spouse," which, as anyone can plainly see, is not the same thing at all as " husband" must support "wife." Now, under Colorado law, the wife shares equally the obligation to support her family, under pain of criminal conviction as a Class 5 felony.

All this specific legislation supported by the ERA proponents in the various state legislatures proves that—despite their denials when they are talking in the press—ERA proponents are working assiduously to make the financial obligation for family support fall equally on the wife, and to deprive the wife of her present legal right to be supported by her husband.

The injustice of this was demonstrated anew by a Pennsylvania court decision on April 2, 1975, involving a bastardy case. Under the new Pennsylvania state equal rights amendment, the court ruled unconstitutional the Pennsylvania law requiring the father of an illegitimate child to pay the financial expenses and support of the baby. The court voided that law under ERA because it imposes a heavier obligation on the father than on the mother.

So, the woman bears the baby, and the man gets off scot-free. That is the inescapable result of ERA because ERA cannot change the fact of which sex gets pregnant, but ERA can and does change the law about who is responsible for financial support. This is what the ERA proponents are working hard for in the legislatures and in the courts—all the time they are denying this when they speak in the press or to audiences of married women.

Homosexual Rights

When ERA proponents are speaking before women's clubs that are reasonably strait-laced and proper, they deny that ERA will grant homosexuals all the rights that now belong to husbands and wives, and profess horror that anyone would use "scare tactics" by mentioning this subject. But when ERA proponents speak before lawyers or respond under cross-examination at state hearings, ERA proponents must admit that ERA will legalize homosexual marriages and give homosexuals and lesbians all the rights of husbands and wives such as the right to file joint income tax returns, to adopt children, to teach in the schools, etc.

121

Thus, Rita Hauser, New York lawyer and U.S. representative to the UN Human Rights Commission, addressed the American Bar Association at its annual meeting in St. Louis in August 1970 on the subject of ERA and stated, "I also believe that the proposed Amendment, if adopted, would void the legal requirement or practice of the states' limiting marriage, which is a legal right, to partners of different sexes."

At the Texas hearing on rescission of ratification of ERA, held on April 4, 1975, the ERA proponents provided five constitutional lawyers as their witnesses. Four out of five admitted that ERA will legalize homosexual marriages and give them the rights of husbands and wives. The reason for this is clear. ERA would constitutionally forbid any discrimination "on account of sex," and it is precisely "on account of sex" that a state now denies a marriage license to a man and a man, or to a woman and a woman.

The Federal Grab for Power

When talking before women's groups and the press, the ERA proponents vigorously deny that Section 2 of ERA is a grab for power at the federal level. Section 2 says that Congress shall have the power to enforce ERA. However, under cross-examination at state legislative hearings, the ERA proponents must admit that Section 2, indeed, will authorize Congress, the federal bureaucracy, and the federal courts to intervene to impose their interpretation of "equal rights" on all of us.

Thus, Congresswoman Martha Griffiths, in testifying before the Missouri hearing on January 28, 1975, admitted under cross-examination, "The intent of Section 2 is to make state laws uniform."

"Uniformity" in state laws, of course, is not our American system of government. We have differences among state laws in regard to taxes, criminal laws, property laws, contract laws, election laws, etc. If you don't like the high taxes and high crime rate in New York, you are free to move to a low-tax and low-crime state.

Most of the 16 states that have rejected ERA have state laws that give wives superior rights which they will lose if ERA is ratified. These superior rights, which vary from state to state, include the right of a wife to inherit a large part of her husband's property while she has the right to dispose of her property as she wishes, and the immunity a wife has from her husband's debts while he has no such immunity from her debts.

Florida has a law that gives a small tax advantage to widows, and this superior right was recently upheld by the U.S. Supreme Court. ERA will, of course, wipe this out. It is a measure of the hypocrisy of the ERA proponents that their lawyers cite this case in other state hearings as an example of the "injustices" that ERA will get rid of. ERA proponents do not, of course, use this example when they are speaking in Florida.

ERA proponents try to allay the fears of those who worry about the long-term effect of Section 2 by saying that Section 3 gives the state legislatures two years in which to bring their state laws into line. Estimates of the number of state laws in each state that would have to be changed under ERA range from 150 to 400. But under cross-examination, ERA proponents must admit that, if the state legislatures don't conform within the two-year period, then the federal government (either through Congress or the bureaucracy or the courts) will step in and require equality on the terms that the federal government determines.

ERA is thus a tremendous transferal of power from the states to the federal government, and a possible two-year delay in enforcement will not change that fact.

Abortion

Before the general public and pro-life audiences, ERA proponents deny that ERA has anything to do with abortion, and again profess horror and amazement that anyone would try to link the two issues. But when they are testifying before legislative hearings, it is a different story.

Thus, when Sarah Weddington, the ERA leader in the Texas legislature and the lawyer who argued the case in the U.S. Supreme Court for the abortionists, testified before a U.S. Senate Subcommittee on April 11, 1975, she said that enactment of the proposed Human Life Amendment would deny the ERA principle that women have a right to "all choices." That is the code expression for abortion—just as "different lifestyles" and "the right to be different" are the code words for homosexuals.

When Congresswoman Bella Abzug talks about "the constitutional right of females to terminate pregnancies that they do not wish to continue," she is talking about the effect of ERA. There is no such "constitutional right" today. There is only the "Supreme Court right" which flows from the split Roe v. Wade decision of January 22, 1973. The abortionists are confidently expecting that ERA will "constitutionalize" this decision and make it impossible to overturn.

Chapter 13
Who Will Profit from ERA?
July 1975

The state legislative hearings have conclusively proven that there is no affirmative case for ERA. It will give women no new rights, benefits, or opportunities. Every argument that the ERA proponents make before women's groups and in the press can be fully demonstrated to be false, obsolete, or irrelevant.

Why, then, is there such a tremendously well-organized and well-financed drive for ERA? Who, really, will benefit? Or, in the famous Latin phrase, cui bono? Women will lose, families will lose, society will lose—but certain militant minority pressure groups will profit, and that is where the money and push come from.

1. Government employees, particularly federal employees. Certain federal payrollers see in ERA a tremendous opportunity to increase their jurisdiction, their control over our lives and activities, the size of their staffs, and the amount of tax money they have available to spend. Section 2 of ERA is a gigantic grab for power into the hands of the government. This is why so much federal and state tax money is now being spent to push passage of ERA before too many people find out about its dangers.

It is rather well known that the American people have reached just about the maximum of the tax load that they are willing to bear. Every time they get a chance to vote against higher taxes, tax increases are defeated. The advocates of more spending and control by the government are desperate to find new sources of revenue. If they can get all the women out of the homes and into paid employment, this will give the government an enormous new source of additional tax revenue.

2. The homosexuals and the lesbians. Every gay group in the country is supporting speedy ratification of ERA because they see in ERA the chance to get all the rights that husbands and wives now enjoy. Homosexuals have generally been unable to obtain these benefits through the normal legislative process at the Congressional, state, or local level. ERA will make it constitutionally impermissible to discriminate on account of sex, and make it constitutionally impossible to deny their radical demands.

3. The abortionists. The drive for unrestricted, unregulated, and government-financed abortion is the major objective of the women's liberation movement. They look upon a woman's susceptibility to becoming pregnant as the greatest of all injustices between men and women, and they look to the Constitution to remedy the centuries of "oppression" caused by this biological fact. They support ERA as the essential step in establishing abortion as an act that is constitutionally and psychologically normal. All abortionists support ERA.

4. The population-control advocates. The powerful lobby working for Zero Population Growth supports ERA for the reason

that it will have the long-term result of pushing wives out of the homes into the work force, and this will result in their having fewer children. The Rockefeller Commission on Population Growth, which has been a major source of funding for the population control lobby, has made this clear. In its 1970 report, the Rockefeller Commission urged the adoption of ERA for the reason that it will "neutralize the legal, social, and institutional pressures that historically have encouraged childbearing."

5. The radical groups seeking to force the churches to ordain women and admit them to the seminaries in equal numbers with men. Churches today have full freedom of choice; they can ordain or not ordain women, as they wish and as their doctrine teaches. This is not acceptable to the radical women's libbers. They want to use the power of the federal government to force the churches to stop "discriminating" against women and force them to start ordaining women—or else forfeit their tax exemption. They are planning endless litigation against church officials in every denomination, if they decline to acquiesce in the demands of the radical minority.

6. Those who want to weaken our military defenses. ERA will absolutely require the military to remove its quota on the percentage of women, to take women in equal numbers with the men, and to assign women indiscriminately to all jobs including combat. ERA will require the military academies to admit women on a 50/50 basis; ERA will not tolerate "tokenism" as is envisioned by the laws presently proposed in Congress. ERA will require a 50/50 coed army and navy.

Chapter 14
ERA & Women's Colleges
February 1976

Among the many choices available to American women today is the opportunity to attend either a coed or an all-women's college. That right to choose will become a thing of the past if the Equal Rights Amendment is ever ratified.

Why is this so? Because an all-women's single-sex college, by definition, discriminates in its admissions policy on account of sex, and that would not be permitted under ERA. The proposed Equal Rights Amendment, Section 1, states its mandate in clear, absolute, no-exceptions-allowed language:

"Equality of rights under the law shall not be denied or abridged by the United States or by any state on account of sex."

The words "by the United States or by any state" apply to every educational institution which receives any federal or state funding. This specifically includes:

1) all state and federal colleges and universities, and

2) all private colleges and universities that receive any federal or state funds (which is about 98 percent of them and includes practically all the well-known institutions).

If ERA is ever ratified, we are sure to have aggressive federal enforcement by Congress, HEW, and the U.S. Supreme Court because Section 2 states:

"The Congress shall have the power to enforce, by appropriate legislation, the provisions of this article."

Conform or Forfeit

If ERA is ever ratified, therefore, the few remaining state and federal single-sex colleges and universities will be required to go 50/50 coed, and all private colleges and universities will be required to go 50/50 coed or forfeit all their state and federal funding.

This ERA-enforced coed rule would apply to such well-known women's colleges as Smith, Wellesley, Mount Holyoke, and Bryn Mawr. It is unlikely that they would be willing to give up their federal funding which now accounts for a large portion of their annual income. To abandon federal aid would be a tremendous price to pay to retain the simple right they now enjoy, namely, integrity as an all-women's college.

This effect on single-sex colleges is a sure result of ERA— not a matter of speculation. We know this from our experience with the Education Amendments Act of 1972 and its HEW implementation. The Act provides, "No person in the United States shall, on the basis of sex, be excluded from participation in, be denied the benefits of, or be subjected to discrimination under any educational program or activity receiving federal financial assistance." This has been construed to mean that federal control extends to every education program or activity operated by a school or college which receives or benefits from federal funds, whether or not the program or activity itself receives federal assistance.

This 1972 Act specifically exempts admissions to colleges that have been traditionally single-sex (although everything else connected with those colleges is subject to the non-discrimination mandate).

When you refer back to the text of ERA, you will quickly see that it contains no exceptions; it is absolute. There is no way to put an exception in ERA now. The only way to do this would be to start fresh with a new constitutional amendment.

Further evidence of the coed mandate of ERA is shown in the HEW Regulation implementing the Education Amendments Act of 1972, and in the Pennsylvania court decision under the state ERA requiring girls to compete and practice with boys in all sports including football and wrestling.

It is highly probable that all private secondary schools, colleges and universities—even if they do not receive federal funds—will be required to become coed because: (1) it is current Internal Revenue policy to remove the tax exemption of all schools that discriminate in admissions on the basis of race; and, (2) the women's lib radicals repeatedly confirm that they will litigate to force all private institutions to adopt a sex-neutral admissions policy. Their rationale is, "Tax deductibility, the gift of the American people, should not be given to institutions that discriminate."

The majority of American students prefer coed colleges and universities. But what does it profit us to deprive those who prefer single-sex schools and colleges of their right to make that choice?

I am no particular advocate of women's colleges. I personally attended and prefer coed colleges, and so do most members of my family. However, I do believe in the freedom to choose. Different colleges serve different students with different personal needs.

All those who value free choice should oppose ERA because it will force all colleges into coed conformity to build the unisex society demanded by the women's liberation movement.

Chapter 15
What Really Happened in Houston
December 1977

T he weekend of November 18-21, 1977, in Houston was the decisive turning point in the war between Women's Lib and those who are Pro-Family. Houston was the "Midway" battle that determined which is the winning side.

For those too young to know the significance of "Midway," let us explain that the Battle of Midway Island was the decisive turning point of the World War II conflict with Japan. Most people didn't realize it at the time, because the war continued for three more years. But later, when historians looked back on the course of the war, they saw clearly that the Battle of Midway determined which side would win. The Japanese never recovered from their crucial losses in that battle (four aircraft carriers). Midway was one of the most decisive battles ever fought in all history.

Likewise, the Battle of Houston dealt a crippling blow to the anti-family forces of Women's Lib. The war isn't over. The fight for the Equal Rights Amendment will continue for at least 16 more months (and maybe longer, if the proponents get an extension of time). The fight for a Human Life Amendment will probably continue for years. But there is now no question which side will win.

What happened in Houston proved:

1. That the Pro-Family Americans have the dedication and the determination to win over ERA, over abortion, and over other attacks on the moral, social, and economic integrity of the family.

2. That the Women's Lib movement has sealed its own doom by deliberately hanging around its own neck the albatrosses of abortion, lesbianism, pornography, and Federal control.

Houston was selected by the Commission on International Women's Year as the site of its national women's conference—the big national consciousness-raising session planned to follow the conferences in each of the 50 states. In a weak and unthinking moment, Congress appropriated $5 million of the Federal taxpayers' money to finance those conferences.

But more people came to the Pro-Family Rally held in Houston that same weekend than came to the IWY Conference subsidized at the taxpayers' expense! The Houston Post reported that 20,000 persons came to the Pro-Family Rally on Saturday, November 19. The IWY Conference was held at the Albert Thomas Convention Center, which has a seating capacity of about 9,000, and it was never full. It had large blocks of empty seats most of the time.

Houston: A Media Event

The IWY Conference was really a "media event"—not an authentic convention at all. That means it was staged for the benefit

134

of the media coverage. The entire IWY operation was designed as a charade to go through the motions of state conferences, and then a national conference, where thousands of women would be induced to pass resolutions about women's issues that were pre-planned and pre-written a year and a half ago. The IWY Resolutions were published in June 1976 in the IWY $5 book called "To Form a More Perfect Union."

Then, in order to secure media coverage in Houston, Chairman Bella Abzug and other members of the IWY National Commission put out phony tips to the media that pro-family persons and groups would cause a "confrontation," "disruption," and possibly "physical violence." These predictions didn't have a shred of truth in them. They were merely bait to get the press to travel to Houston.

Every reporter who bothered to check with Phyllis Schlafly ahead of time was told positively that she did not intend to attend the IWY Conference in Houston (because she was deliberately excluded by the IWY), and that absolutely no confrontation, disruption, or even picketing was planned by pro-family women. Every reporter who bothered to check with Phyllis ahead of time was told exactly which resolutions would be passed by the IWY Conference, and exactly by what margins. For the reporters who listened to Phyllis, the IWY Houston event contained no surprises.

But some 2,500 media personnel chose to listen to Abzug's prognosis and traveled to Houston. They found that all IWY functions merely played out a scenario that was pre-scripted long in advance.

The Pro-Family Rally, on the other hand, was a genuinely authentic and exciting event. No one could have possibly predicted that such a large crowd would turn out. Unfortunately, it didn't get the coverage it deserved.

So many pro-family women worked on exposing how the Commission on International Women's Year is working for radical goals at the taxpayers' expense that it is literally impossible to list them all. Because of the informal nature of the pro-family coalition, there are many dedicated women and men who labored long and effectively whose names I do not even know. I wish it were possible to give proper credit to all who deserve it. All we can say is, thanks to everyone who helped!

Pro-Family Rally Attracts 20,000

The Pro-Family Rally at the Astro-Arena on Saturday, November 19, in Houston was one of the most amazing events that ever happened. Some 20,000 people assembled, coming from every state in the Union. Most remarkable was the tremendous personal sacrifice involved in the task of getting there. Thousands of those who attended came by bus and had to travel 20 to 44 hours each way in order to attend that three-hour Rally.

Although the success of the Pro-Family Rally was a team effort that involved many dedicated people, the indispensable leader was Lottie Beth Hobbs. She had the vision to see that the Pro-Family Rally could be accomplished despite almost insurmountable odds. She had the courage to set a goal that appeared to be beyond human

136

reach. She had the determination to do the hard work, and to motivate others to do likewise, so that that goal would be reached. We salute a great lady who saw her "impossible dream" crowned with the glory of success.

Of course, no one could do such a great job alone. Special tribute must be paid to Shirley Curry and Tottie Ellis of Tennessee. Shirley Curry was the first one to say, "We'll bring 500 people from Tennessee." She gave the rest of the country a standard to match and the enthusiasm to motivate them to do it. I'm sure there were moments when she was sorry she had made that commitment, but she over-delivered. Ultimately, 50 buses rolled to Houston from Tennessee.

Dianne Edmondson of Oklahoma was responsible for hundreds, and perhaps thousands, of those who traveled to Houston for the Pro-Family Rally. Her excellent cassette on Women's Lib and its attack on the family was heard by thousands in the months prior to the IWY Conference. It persuaded those women that they could do something constructive for God and Country by attending the Pro-Family Rally in Houston.

Suzanne Thomas deserves our thanks for her skillful and effective job in handling public relations for the Pro-Family Rally and in speaking on the issues in all the media.

Catherine Lemm was of crucial importance to the success of the Pro-Family Rally. Serving as treasurer for the Rally, she handled the contributions, most of which came in dollar bills and even silver. This turned out to be a huge job and required the help of her entire family.

300,000 Pro-Family Petitions

The Pro-Family Rally at the Astro-Arena was an exciting program, well worth the long, tiresome bus trip to Houston. It presented a star line-up of speakers. Lottie Beth Hobbs explained "Why a Pro-Family Rally" and presented the four pro-family resolutions to the overwhelming and enthusiastic approval of the crowd. Attorney Nellie Gray, president of the March for Life, and Dr. Mildred Jefferson, president of the Right-to- Life Federation, both gave eloquent speeches on the right to life of the unborn child. Representative Clay Smothers, Texas legislator, spoke on how society must defend itself against the homosexuals. Elisabeth Elliott, author and missionary, spoke on "Let Me Be A Woman." Phyllis Schlafly spoke on "ERA: An Attack on the Family." Congressman Robert K. Dornan gave the final speech on "Let Your Voice Be Heard in Washington."

The most exciting part of all was when Lottie Beth Hobbs announced that there were 300,000 pro-family petitions massed on the stage, and they are still coming in. The Pro-Family Rally and the pro-family petitions do speak for the majority of Americans.

There were many differences between the Pro-Family Rally at the Astro-Arena and the taxpayer-funded IWY Conference at the Albert Thomas Convention Center. The Pro-Family Rally opened with a prayer, and the asking of God's blessing was part and parcel of the entire program. The IWY Conference did not permit an opening prayer.

At the Pro-Family Rally, there was a beautiful spirit of happy and loving people. They all have their share of life's burdens, handicaps and disappointments; but they have the serenity of knowing that eternal life awaits those who fulfill the mission that God has planned for their lives. The IWY Conference had people who wake up in the morning with a chip on their shoulders, and who are grossly intolerant of any views other than their own.

I must confess that I did not believe a Pro-Family Rally of any important size could ever take place. There were too many obstacles. Houston is so far away from most of the U.S. population. The IWY Conference would be paying the travel expenses of delegates to its conference—but those who attended the Pro-Family Rally would have to dig deep in their pockets to pay their own way. I did not see how as many people could be persuaded to attend the Pro-Family Rally as would be subsidized to attend the IWY Conference. Besides, the IWY officials had reserved every public meeting place and hotel in Houston in order to make it impossible to meet without IWY approval.

But Lottie Beth Hobbs and her associates in the Pro-Family Rally Coalition made the impossible come true—despite all the Doubting Thomases. I am happy to have been proved wrong—and proud to have been invited to participate in their remarkable success.

Houston Proves Radicals and Lesbians Run IWY

There were no surprises in the national conference financed by the Commission on International Women's Year. The IWY state conferences were so rigidly controlled that the IWY had a big majority of delegates dutifully eager to vote as they had been pre-programmed. The principal resolutions passed in Houston were:

1. Ratification of the Equal Rights Amendment. (This has always been the number-one priority of the IWY. At its first official meeting in 1975, the IWY voted unanimously to make ratification of ERA its "highest priority" and resolved "to do all in our capacity to see that the Equal Rights Amendment is ratified at the earliest possible moment.")

2. Privileges for homosexuals and lesbians to teach in the schools, to rent from any landlord, and to have custody of children.

3. Federally-funded abortion on demand; the requirement that abortion be included in privately-financed medical services; and the approval of abortions for teenagers without parental knowledge or consent.

4. The Federal Government should assume a major role in directing and providing funding for comprehensive child care.

Due to the tactics used by the IWY at the various state conferences, including total control of the delegate election machinery and steamroller parliamentary tactics, there were only about 20 percent pro-family delegates among the some 2,000 IWY delegates assembled at the Albert Thomas Convention Center.

The pro-family delegates faithfully fulfilled their commitment to serve in the IWY conference. They sat like ladies in their seats through hour after hour of harassment, procedure instead of substance, pro-ERA propaganda speeches, and sheer boredom. They had to make the biggest sacrifice of all because they remained inside the IWY convention hall listening to offensive speeches or trivial procedure, and enduring the hostility of the lib delegates, while having to miss the fun and inspiration of the Pro-Family Rally. The some 400 pro-family delegates who made that great sacrifice deserve our admiration and thanks.

The Floor Leader of the pro-family delegates was Senator Joan Gubbins, who was also chairman of the Indiana delegation. She and her lieutenants, such as Betty Hanicke, chairman of the Kansas delegation, did a magnificent and dignified job in the face of overwhelming odds and obstacles.

Senator Gubbins and other pro-family delegates made valiant efforts to debate the radical IWY resolutions but were almost uniformly denied this basic right. The IWY conference was designed and planned to prevent substantive debate on the major issues, such as ERA. The IWY conference can be accurately described as a "card play." Hours were spent discussing the different colored cards that had to be held up before delegates could be recognized. This was just a device to allow the IWY chair to control who was recognized at the microphones, and to prevent pro-family delegates from speaking at all. In three days of sessions, pro-family delegates were only allowed to make one one-minute statement against ERA, and two two-minute statements against abortion. Pro-family delegates were not allowed to speak against Federal child care or lesbian privileges.

Most outrageous of all, the IWY Chair refused to allow the pro-family delegates to present their Minority Report. This was a clear violation of all rules of parliamentary procedure and evidence of the intolerance of the IWY toward non-IWY views. Special thanks should be given to Dianne Edmondson and Rosemary Thomson, who drafted the Minority Report of the Pro-Family Coalition which the IWY Conference Chair refused to admit.

Lesbian Arrogance

Anyone who doubts the total commitment of the IWY Commission to homosexuals should get a copy of the official 38-page IWY booklet called "A Lesbian Guide." On the cover it states proudly, "This booklet was prepared by the National Gay Task Force and officially approved by the National Commission on the Observance of International Women's Year."

The IWY permitted the lesbians to display and peddle their booklets, buttons, and devices which were offensive, obscene and pornographic at and near the conference. The lesbian pamphlets openly distributed and sold there included: "What Lesbians Do," "The Playbook for Women About Sex," "High School Sensuality: A Teaching Guide," "Good Vibrations," "Getting in Touch: Self Sexuality for Women," "Our Bodies Ourselves," "The Love My Body Book," and "For Yourself: The Fulfillment of Female Sexuality."

The buttons worn and peddled at the IWY Conference included "Mother Nature is a Lesbian," "Every day is Mother's Day (And I'm Sick and Tired of It)," "Women Stop Giving it Away," "Trust in God, She Will Provide," "Out of the Closet and into the Street," "Ordain Women or Stop Baptizing Them," "F—

142

Housework," "A Woman Without a Man is like a Fish Without a Bicycle," and one about the Pope too indecent to quote here.

It is noteworthy that the IWY Conference failed to include one word of condemnation of the worst exploitation of women— pornography. The reason is obvious: Women's Lib itself has too big a stake in an alliance with pornographers. The lesbian pamphlets are just as pornographic as the smut peddled by the pornography profiteers in the adult bookstores.

Through the months preceding the Houston conference, the IWY Citizens Review Committee, under the chairmanship of Rosemary Thomson of Illinois, and with splendid assistance of Nellie Gray of Washington, D.C., carried on a watchdog effort to expose the irregularities and illegalities of IWY activities. This Committee monitored IWY state conferences, assembled the facts, collected the documentation, and developed a monumental record.

This IWY Citizens Review Committee assisted in getting the witnesses who testified at the Congressional ad hoc hearing chaired by Senator Jesse Helms in Washington, D.C., on September 14 and 15. According to Senator Helms' statement in the Congressional Record of October 3, the testimony of the 70 witnesses who traveled from 40 states at their own expense to relate their experiences with their own state's IWY conference identified the following problems:

1. IWY Coordinating Committees loaded to represent only feminist groups and viewpoints.

2. Hostility and discrimination against non-radical women.

3. Lack of publicity to non-feminist women's groups.

4. Lesbian workshops and pornographic entertainment.

5. Anti-religious activity.

6. Operation MMOPP and fraudulent voting.

7. Parliamentary violations.

8. Railroaded resolutions.

9. Rigged elections and voting irregularities.

10. Lobbying for Equal Rights Amendment and abortion on demand.

Congressman Robert K. Dornan held another Congressional ad hoc hearing on November 18, 1977, at the Ramada Inn Civic Center in Houston in order to hear additional testimony about the illegalities and irregularities connected with the IWY state and national conferences. Again, women attended from many states at their own expense in order to spell out their eyewitness observations of the unfairness, bias, and misuse of Federal funds by the IWY.

Phyllis Schlafly testified about the way the IWY had violated its promises during the original Congressional debate to represent "every point of view," and how the IWY has been in constant violation of the two principal requirements of the Federal Advisory Committee Act (Public Law 92-463), namely, (1) that the membership shall "be fairly balanced in terms of the points of view represented," and (2) that it "not be inappropriately influenced...by any special interest."

A large part of the success of pro-family efforts in Houston was due to the excellent job done by the Eagles in counteracting the dominance of the media by the IWY.

Eagle Forum set up a press headquarters at the Ramada Inn Civic Center in Houston. We had a news conference each morning at

8:30 A.M. participated in by spokesmen for the pro-family coalition. It was a modest but comfortable press room in which we supplied typewriters and telephones for the press.

Our Eagle Public Relations Chairman, Kathleen Teague, who is also Virginia Stop ERA Co-Chairman, gave sound advice and skillfully handled many of the tense press and public relations problems about IWY that arose. Kathy deserves special credit for setting up the initial arrangements in Houston, as well as the press breakfast in Washington, D.C., two weeks before the IWY Conference at which Phyllis was able to explain our opposition to the ERA Extension Bill.

Our Eagle Media Chairman, Elaine Donnelly, who is also Michigan Stop ERA Chairman, did a tremendously effective job. She wrote and printed a press packet to provide background on IWY. She put out many press releases giving our update comment on fast-breaking developments. She arranged press conferences, and skillfully cooperated with the press so that they might cover our views.

Nothing would have been possible in connection with our press operation in Houston without the special dedication of our Headquarters Chairman, Ann McGraw, who is also Missouri Stop ERA Chairman. Ann went to Houston ten days ahead of time to make arrangements and to organize a smooth-running operation. She was assisted by about a dozen other Eagles who gave generously of their time to handle the thousand details that arose.

Finally, special mention must be made of Chris Collins, who served as Literature Chairman in Houston. Chris deserves a merit badge for courage in braving the hostility and rudeness of the libs who harassed her steadily while she manned the table with Eagle Forum and Stop ERA literature.

Chapter 16
How ERA Will Raise Insurance Rates
February 1979

One of the many unforeseen and undesirable effects of the Equal Rights Amendment is the way it will raise the rates of automobile insurance for most Americans, principally for young women age 16 to 25 (and their parents if they pay the premiums). Young women under age 25 pay much lower automobile accident insurance premiums than young men because young men have a much higher rate of accidents.

Since insurance is an industry regulated by state law, the ERA mandate would govern it. ERA would forbid the industry to charge young men more and young women less as a result of a classification by sex. Under ERA, both sexes would have to pay the same rate, which means that young men would pay 8 percent less but young women would pay 29 percent more.

Some people who don't understand insurance ask the question, why not charge rates based on which individuals have the accidents? But if the insurance companies know who will have the accidents, they will simply refuse to sell insurance to those individuals or charge them what their accidents actually cost. The whole principle of insurance is based on distributing the risk among groups in which the average cost can be statistically and reliably predicted. This is the system that charges everyone a reasonable rate and prevents any one individual from being ruined by a $100,000 accident.

The ERA, if ratified into the U.S. Constitution, will prohibit any difference of treatment "on account of sex." ERA cannot change the statistical fact that young men on the average have many more accidents and therefore cost more to insure. But ERA would require insurance companies to pretend that this difference does not exist and to treat males and females the same.

Some people might be inclined to think that, if a bona fide sex difference could be statistically proved, the U.S. Supreme Court would allow the different rates to continue. This argument was conclusively eliminated by the U.S. Supreme Court in the 1978 case of Los Angeles v. Manhart.

In that case, the issue was whether the city of Los Angeles could charge women employees more for payments into a pension plan since it is a proven statistical fact that women live longer after retirement than men, and therefore their pensions cost more.

The Supreme Court answered no. The Court ruled that, even though the pension plan was based on a factual difference in longevity between women and men, it ended up as a difference of treatment on account of sex, and therefore is "sex discrimination" prohibited under Title VII of the Civil Rights Act, which applies to nearly all employers.

The Manhart case applies only to pensions governed by Title VII. The ERA, if it ever becomes part of the Constitution, would apply to all areas including automobile accident insurance and life insurance. Life insurance is another area where women receive more favorable treatment. Women now pay lower life insurance rates than men because women live longer.

There is another item to note. Remember, ERA does not use the words "on account of gender" or even the word "women." It says, "on account of sex." The women's lib movement usually argues that "sex discrimination" not only includes a difference of treatment based on gender, but also on marital status. "Sex" is a word with many meanings, and it is not defined in ERA. It is therefore possible that ERA would prohibit insurance companies from charging different rates for married persons and unmarried persons. If different rates based on marital status are prohibited by ERA, rates on married males under age 25 would go up 68 percent while the rates on unmarried males under 25 would go down 9 percent.

Thus ERA would substantially raise the automobile accident rates on most Americans. It would require groups with good accident records to subsidize groups with bad accident records. And like nearly everything else about ERA, those who would lose the most would be women and married couples.

Chapter 17
Ruth Bader Ginsburg's Feminist World View
July 1993

How does it happen that a Supreme Court nominee whose only experience in private law practice was seven years as general counsel to the ACLU came to be praised by almost everyone as a "moderate" and a "centrist"?

My theory is this just proves how easily men are fooled by a skirt. They deduced that Ruth Bader Ginsburg is "moderate" because she isn't a loud-mouthed, frizzy-haired, bra-burning, street demonstrator.

In fact, Ginsburg's writings betray her as a radical, doctrinaire feminist, far out of the mainstream. She shares the chip-on-the-shoulder, radical feminist view that American women have endured centuries of oppression and mistreatment from men. That's why, in her legal writings, she self-identifies with feminist Sarah Grimke's statement, "All I ask of our brethren is that they take their feet off our necks," and with feminist Simone de Beauvoir's put-down of women as "the second sex." (De Beauvoir's most famous quote is, "Marriage is an obscene bourgeois institution.")

In a speech published by the *Phi Beta Kappa Key Reporter* in 1974, Ginsburg called for affirmative action hiring quotas for career women, using the police as an example in point. She said, "Affirmative action is called for in this situation."

On the other hand, she considered it a setback for "women's rights" when the Supreme Court, in Kahn v. Shevin (1974), upheld a Florida property tax exemption for widows. Ginsburg disdains what she calls "traditional sex roles" and demands strict gender neutrality (except, of course, for quota hiring of career women).

Ginsburg's real claim to her status as the premier feminist lawyer is her success in winning the 1973 Supreme Court case Frontiero v. Richardson, which she unabashedly praised as an "activist" decision. She obviously shares the view of Justice William Brennan's opinion that American men, "in practical effect, put women, not on a pedestal, but in a cage," and that "throughout much of the 19th century the position of women in our society was, in many respects, comparable to that of blacks under the pre-Civil War slave codes."

A typical feminist, Ruth Bader Ginsburg wants affirmative action quota hiring for career women but at the same time wants to wipe out the special rights that state laws traditionally gave to wives.

Anyone who thinks that American women in the 19th century were treated like slaves, and in the 20th century were kept in a "cage," has a world view that is downright dangerous to have on the U.S. Supreme Court. She's another Brennan, and no conservative should vote to confirm her.

Of course, Ginsburg passed President Clinton's self-proclaimed litmus test for appointment to the Supreme Court—she is "pro-choice." But that's not all; she wants to write taxpayer funding of abortions into the U.S. Constitution, something that 72 percent of Americans oppose and even the pro-abortion, pro-Roe v. Wade Supreme Court refused to do.

It has been considered settled law since the Supreme Court decisions in a trilogy of cases in 1977 (Beal v. Doe, Maher v. Roe, and Poelker v. Doe) that the Constitution does not compel states to pay for abortions. These cases were followed by the 1980 Supreme Court decision of Harris v. McRae upholding the Hyde Amendment's ban on spending federal taxpayers' money for abortions. The Court ruled that "it simply does not follow that a woman's freedom of choice [to have an abortion] carries with it a constitutional entitlement to the financial resources to avail herself of the full range of protected choices."

Ginsburg has planted herself firmly in opposition to this settled law. In a 1980 book entitled *Constitutional Government in America,* Judge Ginsburg wrote a chapter endorsing taxpayer funding of abortions as a constitutional right and condemning the High Court's rulings.

"This was the year the women lost," Ginsburg wrote in her analysis of the 1977 cases. "Most unsettling of the losses are the decisions on access by the poor to elective abortions." Criticizing the 6-to-3 majority in the funding cases, Ginsburg asserted that "restrictions on public funding and access to public hospitals for poor women" were a retreat from Roe v. Wade, as well as a "stunning curtailment" of women's rights.

The phony "concern" expressed by pro-abortion lobbyists like Kate Michelman is just a smokescreen. Ginsburg's article criticizing Roe v. Wade, which has received some attention since her nomination, merely complained that the Court didn't adopt the "women's equality" theory that she had personally developed in the 1970s. Ginsburg's article was not a legal criticism, but a political one: if the Court had been less categorical in its Roe language, she said, it would not have provoked the "well-organized and vocal right-to-life movement." Ginsburg preferred to legalize abortion with arcane and obtuse legal gobbledegook that didn't agitate the grassroots.

Feminists Want to Change Our Laws

Ruth Bader Ginsburg is a longtime advocate of the extremist feminist notion that any differentiation whatsoever on account of gender should be unconstitutional. Her radical views are made clear in a book called *Sex Bias in the U.S. Code*, which she co-authored in 1977 with another feminist, Brenda Feigen-Fasteau, for which they were paid with federal funds under Contract No. CR3AK010.

Sex Bias in the U.S. Code, published by the U.S. Commission on Civil Rights, was the source of the claim widely made in the 1970s that 800 federal laws "discriminated" on account of sex. The 230-page book was written to identify those laws and to recommend the specific changes demanded by the feminist movement in order to conform to the "equality principle" and promote ratification of the Equal Rights Amendment, for which Ginsburg was a fervent advocate. (The ERA died in 1982.)

Sex Bias in the U.S. Code is a handbook which shows how the feminists want to change our laws, our institutions and our attitudes, and convert America into a "gender-free" society. It clearly shows that the feminists are not trying to redress any legitimate grievances women might have, but want to change human nature, social mores, and relationships between men and women—and want to do that by changing our laws. Despite the noisy complaints of the feminists about the oppression of women, a combing of federal laws by Ruth Bader Ginsburg, then a Columbia University Law School professor, and her staff under a federal grant of tax dollars, unearthed no federal laws that harm women! The feminists' complaints about "discriminatory laws" are either ridiculous or offensive.

Here are some of the extremist feminist concepts from the Ginsburg book, *Sex Bias in the U.S. Code*.

In the Family

1. The traditional family concept of husband as breadwinner and wife as homemaker must be eliminated.

"Congress and the President should direct their attention to the concept that pervades the Code: that the adult world is (and should be) divided into two classes—independent men, whose primary responsibility is to win bread for a family, and dependent women, whose primary responsibility is to care for children and household. This concept must be eliminated from the code if it is to reflect the equality principle." (p. 206)

"It is a prime recommendation of this report that all legislation based on the breadwinning, husband-dependent, homemaking-wife pattern be recast using precise functional description in lieu of gross gender classification." (p. 212)

"A scheme built upon the breadwinning husband [and] dependent homemaking wife concept inevitably treats the woman's efforts or aspirations in the economic sector as less important than the man's." (p. 209)

2. The Federal Government must provide comprehensive government child-care.

"The increasingly common two-earner family pattern should impel development of a comprehensive program of government-supported child care." (p. 214)

3. The right to determine the family residence must be taken away from the husband.

"Title 43 provisions on homestead rights of married couples are premised on the assumption that a husband is authorized to determine the family's residence. This 'husband's prerogative' is obsolete." (p. 214)

4. Homestead law must give twice as much benefit to couples who live apart from each other as to a husband and wife who live together.

"Married couples who choose to live together would be able to enter upon only one tract at a time." (p. 175) "Couples willing to live apart could make entry on two tracts." (p. 176)

5. No-fault divorce must be adopted nationally.

"Consideration should be given to revision of 38 U.S.C. §101(3) to reflect the trend toward no-fault divorce." (p. 159) "Retention of a fault concept in provisions referring to separation…is questionable in light of the trend away from fault determinations in the dissolution of marriages." (pp. 214-215)

6. The government must provide "paternity" leave for childrearing as well as maternity leave.

"A provision of Title 20 (§904) authorizes 'maternity' leave. To the extent that leave is authorized for childrearing as distinguished from childbearing, fathers as well as mothers should be eligible." (p. 213)

7. The role of motherhood must be restricted to the very few months in which a woman is pregnant and nursing her baby, because having a baby is just a temporary disability (like breaking a leg, which requires a six-week cast). Mothers are not entitled to any special benefits or protections for motherhood responsibilities beyond those limited weeks.

"The references are to 'maternal' health or welfare and 'mothers.' Those terms would be appropriately descriptive only if the programs involved were confined to care for pregnant women and lactating mothers." (p. 212)

8. The law must not assume that a woman takes her husband's name upon remarriage.

"38 U.S.C. §3020 prohibits delivery of benefit checks to 'widows' [of veterans] whom the postal employee believes to have remarried, 'unless the mail is addressed to such widow in the name she has acquired by her remarriage.' As written, the provision implies that women automatically acquire a new name upon remarriage, an implication inconsistent with current law and the equality principle." (p. 156)

In the Military

1. Women must be drafted when men are drafted.

"Supporters of the equal rights principle firmly reject draft or combat exemption for women, as Congress did when it refused to qualify the Equal Rights Amendment by incorporating any military service exemption. The equal rights principle implies that women must be subject to the draft if men are, that military assignments must be made on the basis of individual capacity rather than sex." (p. 218)

"Equal rights and responsibilities for men and women implies that women must be subject to draft registration..." (p. 202)

2. Women must be assigned to military combat duty.

"Until the combat exclusion for women is eliminated, women who choose to pursue a career in the military will continue to be held back by restrictions unrelated to their individual abilities. Implementation of the equal rights principle requires a unitary system of appointment, assignment, promotion, discharge, and retirement, a system that cannot be founded on a combat exclusion for women." (p. 26)

3. Affirmative action must be applied to equalize the number of men and women in the armed services.

"The need for affirmative action and for transition measures is particularly strong in the uniformed services." (p. 218)

In Moral Standards

1. The age of consent for sexual acts must be lowered to 12 years old.

"Eliminate the phrase 'carnal knowledge of any female, not his wife, who has not attained the age of 16 years' and substitute a federal, sex-neutral definition of the offense...A person is guilty of an offense if he engages in a sexual act with another person...[and] the other person is, in fact, less than 12 years old." (p. 102)

2. Bigamists must have special privileges that other felons don't have.

"This section restricts certain rights, including the right to vote or hold office, of bigamists, persons 'cohabiting with more than one woman,' and women cohabiting with a bigamist. Apart from the male/female differentials, the provision is of questionable constitutionality since it appears to encroach impermissibly upon private relationships." (pp. 195-196)

3. Prostitution must be legalized; it is not sufficient to change the law to sex-neutral language.

"Prostitution proscriptions are subject to several constitutional and policy objections. Prostitution, as a consensual act between adults, is arguably within the zone of privacy protected by recent constitutional decisions." (p. 97)

"Retaining prostitution business as a crime in a criminal code is open to debate. Reliable studies indicate that prostitution is not a major factor in the spread of venereal disease, and that prostitution plays a small and declining role in organized crime operations." (p. 99)

"Current provisions dealing with statutory rape, rape, and prostitution are discriminatory on their face…There is a growing national movement recommending unqualified decriminalization [of prostitution] as sound policy, implementing equal rights and individual privacy principles." (pp. 215-216)

4. The Mann Act must be repealed; women should not be protected from "bad" men.

"The Mann Act…prohibits the transportation of women and girls for prostitution, debauchery, or any other immoral purpose. The act poses the invasion of privacy issue in an acute form. The Mann Act also is offensive because of the image of women it perpetuates …It was meant to protect from 'the villainous interstate and international traffic in women and girls,' 'those women and girls who, if given a fair chance, would, in all human probability, have been good wives and mothers and useful citizens…The act was meant to protect weak women from bad men." (pp. 98-99)

5. Prisons and reformatories must be sex-integrated.

"If the grand design of such institutions is to prepare inmates for return to the community as persons equipped to benefit from and contribute to civil society, then perpetuation of single-sex institutions should be rejected…18 U.S.C. §4082, ordering the Attorney General to commit convicted offenders to 'available suitable, and appropriate' institutions, is not sex discriminatory on its face. It should not be applied…to permit consideration of a person's gender as a factor making a particular institution appropriate or suitable for that person." (p. 101)

6. In the merchant marine, provisions for passenger accommodations must be sex-neutralized, and women may not have more bathrooms than men.

"46 U.S.C. §152 establishes different regulations for male and female occupancy of double berths, confines male passengers without wives to the 'forepart' of the vessel, and segregates unmarried females in a separate and closed compartment. 46 U.S.C. §153 requires provision of a bathroom for every 100 male passengers for their exclusive use and one for every 50 female passengers for the exclusive use of females and young children." (p. 190)

"46 U.S.C. §152 might be changed to allow double occupancy by two 'consenting adults.'…Requirements for separate bathroom facilities stipulated in Section 153 should be retained but equalized so that the ratio of persons to facility is not sex-determined." (p. 192)

In Education

1. Single-sex schools and colleges, and single-sex school and college activities must be sex-integrated.

"The equal rights principle looks toward a world in which men and women function as full and equal partners, with artificial barriers removed and opportunity unaffected by a person's gender.

Preparation for such a world requires elimination of sex separation in all public institutions where education and training occur." (p. 101)

2. All-boys' and all-girls' organizations must be sex-integrated because separate-but-equal organizations perpetuate stereotyped sex roles.

"Societies established by Congress to aid and educate young people on their way to adulthood should be geared toward a world in which equal opportunity for men and women is a fundamental principle. The educational purpose would be served best by immediately extending membership to both sexes in a single organization." (pp. 219-220)

3. Fraternities and sororities must be sex-integrated.

"Replace college fraternity and sorority chapters with college 'social societies.'" (p. 169)

4. The Boy Scouts, the Girl Scouts, and other Congressionally-chartered youth organizations, must change their names and their purposes and become sex-integrated.

"Six organizations, which restrict membership to one sex, furnish educational, financial, social and other assistance to their young members. These include the Boy Scouts, the Girl Scouts, Future Farmers of America...Boys' Clubs of America...Big Brothers of America...and the Naval Sea Cadets Corps...The Boy Scouts and Girl Scouts, while ostensibly providing 'separate but equal' benefits to both sexes, perpetuate stereotyped sex roles to the extent that they carry out congressionally-mandated purposes. 36 U.S.C. §23 defines the purpose of the Boy Scouts as the promotion of...the ability of boys to do things for themselves and others, to train them in scoutcraft, and to teach them patriotism, courage, self-reliance, and kindred virtues…The purpose of the Girl Scouts, on the other hand, is '…to promote the qualities of truth, loyalty, helpfulness, friendliness, courtesy, purity, kindness, obedience, cheerfulness, thriftiness, and kindred virtues among girls, as a preparation for their responsibilities in the home and for service to the community…' (36 U.S.C. §33.)" (pp. 145-146)

"Organizations that bestow material benefits on their members should consider a name change to reflect extension of membership to both sexes…[and] should be revised to conform to these changes. Review of the purposes and activities of all these clubs should be undertaken to determine whether they perpetuate sex-role stereotypes." (pp. 147-148)

5. The 4-H Boys and Girls Clubs must be sex-integrated into 4-H Youth Clubs.

"Change in the proper name '4-H Boys and Girls Clubs' should reflect consolidation of the clubs to eliminate sex segregation, e.g., '4-H-Youth Clubs.'" (p. 138)

6. Men and women should be required to salute the flag in the same way.

"Differences [between men and women] in the authorized method of saluting the flag should be eliminated in 36 U.S.C. §177." (p. 148)

In Language

1. About 750 of the 800 federal laws that allegedly "discriminate" on account of sex merely involve the use of so-called "sexist" words which the ERAers wanted to censor out of the English language. Sex Bias even demands bad grammar to appease the feminists: "All federal statutes, regulations, and rules shall [use] plural constructions to avoid third person singular pronouns." (pp. 52-53)

2. In another piece of silliness, Sex Bias demands that Congress create a female anti-litter symbol to match "Johnny Horizon."

"A further unwarranted male reference...regulates use of the 'Johnny Horizon' anti-litter symbol...This sex stereotype of the outdoorsperson and protector of the environment should be supplemented with a female figure promoting the same values. The two figures should be depicted as persons of equal strength of character, displaying equal familiarity and concern with the terrain of our country." (p. 100)

3. On the other hand, Sex Bias shows its hypocrisy by demanding that the "Women's Bureau" in the U.S. Department of Labor be continued. Although the authors admit that this is "inappropriate" (it is obviously sex discriminatory), they simply demand it anyway. "The Women's Bureau is...a necessary and proper office for service during a transition period until the equal rights principle is realized." (p. 221)

4. *Sex Bias in the U.S. Code* makes a fundamental error in stating, "The Constitution, which provides the framework for the American legal system, was drafted using the generic term 'man.'" (p. 2) The word "man" does not appear in the U.S. Constitution (except in a no-longer-operative section of the 14th Amendment, which is not in effect now and was not in effect when the Constitution was "drafted"). The U.S. Constitution is a beautiful sex-neutral document. It exclusively uses sex-neutral words such as person, citizen, resident, inhabitant, President, Vice President, Senator, Representative, elector, Ambassador, and minister, so that women enjoy every constitutional right that men enjoy—and always have.

Sex Bias in the U.S. Code proves that Ruth Bader Ginsburg's "equality principle" would bring about extremist changes in our legal, political, social, and educational structures. The feminists are working hard—with our tax dollars—to bring this about by constitutional mandate (through the Equal Rights Amendment) or by legislative changes or by judicial activism. Ruth Bader Ginsburg has been their premier lawyer for two decades.

Finally, who but an embittered feminist could have said what Ruth Bader Ginsburg said when she stood beside President Clinton in the Rose Garden the day of her nomination for the Supreme Court: She wished that her mother had "lived in an age when daughters are cherished as much as sons." Where in the world has Ginsburg been living? In China? In India? Her statement was an insult to all American parents who do, indeed, cherish their daughters as much as their sons.

164

About Phyllis Schlafly

Remarks delivered by John Schlafly at the funeral of his mother, Phyllis Schlafly, at the Cathedral Basilica of St. Louis on September 10, 2016:

When my father, Fred Schlafly, reached the age of 75, and realized he could no longer compete in the sports he had enjoyed throughout his life, he turned to my mother one day and said, "Phyllis, you probably have about 10 good years left."

That conversation took place more than 30 years ago. And those 30 extra years were good years: good for us, of course, her family and friends who received her wise counsel; and also good for our country, as her political activism continued to influence the 2016 election.

They were good years for Phyllis, too, despite the increasing burdens of her old age. She was able to watch her family grow to 25 descendants, with more on the way. In her final days, she had the great joy of seeing the infants and toddlers that my father never knew.

My parents were partners in their life together, and Phyllis depended on Fred for everyday reinforcement. He supported her career, screened what she wrote, and coached her on what to say. She called him "the censor."

Fred Schlafly's influence is apparent in Phyllis' most widely read article, "What's Wrong With 'Equal Rights' for Women?" First published in February 1972, that article has since been reprinted in dozens of college textbooks and is considered the classic expression of Phyllis' opposition to feminism.

The 1972 article set forth the proposition that our public laws and policies, as embedded in the fundamental law of our nation, should reinforce the family as the basic unit of any society. Confronting the burgeoning feminist movement and its principal objective, the Equal Rights Amendment (ERA), Phyllis' simple but powerful argument seemed controversial and even retrograde to liberals.

As Father Brian Harrison explained in his homily today, the idea that a nation's laws should recognize the basic social unit as the family, rather than the individual, is grounded in the social teaching of the Catholic church. It's the central insight of the pope's famous 1891 encyclical Rerum Novarum, which launched Catholic social teaching, and it has been reaffirmed many times since then.

Phyllis expressed the idea in a way that attracted tens of thousands of people, mostly of other faiths, to what she called the "pro-family" movement. Many of those she touched and inspired have honored our family by coming here today.

We now take Phyllis to rest beside her husband, my father, in the place she selected many years ago. Like every place she ever lived, she decided the burial plot needed another tree—a maple tree that that turns bright gold in the fall.

She selected a tree, planted it and drove there frequently with buckets of water, to make sure the tree survived. Since we buried my father there, 23 years ago, the little tree that Phyllis planted has become a powerful, majestic, stately canopy, and next month its color will be gorgeous.

Reflecting on my mother's long life, the singular quality that explains her effectiveness is that she was <u>always</u> prepared. Whether her task was to give a speech, conduct a meeting, or meet a deadline, her careful preparation made the job seem effortless and gave her time to deal with unexpected events.

Phyllis was never at a loss for the appropriate words. She faced crisis and conflict with grace, and she infuriated opponents with her unflappable good humor.

In the parable of the bridegroom (Matt. 25:1-13), Jesus tells the story of 10 women who were called to light the way for a wedding party. Five of the women brought no extra oil, and their lamps went out before the wedding party arrived.

The other five women came prepared with extra oil in case the wedding party was running late. The sensible five were admitted to the wedding feast from which the foolish five were excluded.

Phyllis would have been one of the five wise enough to bring an extra flask of oil. Even in her final year, she was planning for the future, including America's future as well as her own.

Phyllis Schlafly was a wise woman, a sensible woman, a faithful woman. Her lamp would not go out, and I believe she was prepared for today.

Phyllis Schlafly, 1924-2016 by Andy Schlafly, September 13, 2016

Phyllis Schlafly was with us a glorious 92 years, and active in politics for more than 70 of them. It is difficult to identify any issue that she was not on the right side of, typically years or decades before others rallied beside her.

She wrote or spoke out on nearly every controversial American political matter, and the conservative movement today is based largely on work that she did five, ten, twenty, and even sixty years ago. Though we grieve her passing, she leaves us with a legacy that will take us our own lifetimes to fully appreciate.

Donald Trump, in his remarkable eulogy to Phyllis last Saturday at the beginning of her funeral, observed that Phyllis has shaped American politics for more than one-quarter of its entire existence. He commented that she always put America first, as he does, and the massive crowd of attendees gave a standing ovation to Trump in immense gratitude to him for so honoring Phyllis.

Phyllis wrote a bestselling book in 1964 called *A Choice Not An Echo*, which foreshadowed Trump's meteoric rise. The book exposed how the political system is rigged by kingmakers, and she was thrilled by the arrival of Trump as a candidate for president, 52 years after publication of her work, to take on and defeat the kingmakers in the Republican Party.

Phyllis anticipated and led on so many political issues that it would require another book just to list them. Her *Phyllis Schlafly Report*, now in its 50th year, is probably the longest continuing political newsletter in history, and its inaugural edition discussed the

168

importance of our Panama Canal a full decade before that became a hot issue propelling Ronald Reagan to his successful campaign for president.

In defeating the Equal Rights Amendment, the work for which Phyllis is most famous, she took an initially unpopular stance years before others joined her. Her successful STOP ERA effort did more to define the conservative movement today than any other struggle.

But unlike most political leaders, Phyllis also had a tremendous cultural influence, by establishing respectability for those who stay at home and raise their children. Even many liberal-leaning women who attained adulthood in the 1980s and beyond are grateful to Phyllis for carving out space in our culture for them to spend some time away from the rat race to raise their children, and educate them at home.

Indeed, one of Phyllis's proudest achievements was that she taught her children how to read at home, which she did for all six of them in the 1950s and 1960s. This was decades before the homeschooling movement blossomed as an expansion on the same concept.

Recently some have called Phyllis the "Iron Lady," but that term fails to capture the enormous good humor and charm that she always had in the face of intense hostility. Many middle-aged people today had the benefit of attending a debate or presentation by Phyllis on a college campus, where she would invariably withstand a hostile opponent or audience with remarkable grace.

The funeral Mass on Saturday was held at the Cathedral Basilica in St. Louis, the same place where Phyllis was married in 1949 to Fred Schlafly, a blissful union that lasted until his death in 1993. But far from slowing down as a widow, Phyllis continued her work for another 23 years by both building on her prior efforts and expanding into new topics.

For example, she wrote her book on *The Supremacists* in 2004 to explain the growing problem of judicial supremacy, which foreshadowed the shocking court decisions in recent years and the crisis that we face in this election as the replacement for Justice Scalia hinges on the outcome. Her more recent book on *No Higher Power: Obama's War on Religious Freedom* (2012) exposed the anti-Christian agenda of the Obama Administration.

Phyllis attended Republican National Conventions over a span of 64 years, from 1952 to 2016, and I had the joy of being with her for nearly two weeks in Cleveland this summer at her final convention. The party platform now embraces Phyllis's positions on everything from building a wall to stop illegal immigration, to being strongly pro-life, to attaining military superiority, which were all positions that she staked out decades ago.

Phyllis never stopped writing, speaking, and organizing. The very day after her passing away on September 5th, the anniversary of Mother Teresa's death, Phyllis' 27th book was released: *The Conservative Case for Trump*.

William Shakespeare left this world with a legacy in playwriting that took generations to admire fully. Phyllis Schlafly produced more during her lifetime than the rest of us could keep up with, and it may take us decades simply to realize all the good work that Phyllis, the "conservative hero" in the words of Trump's eulogy, has left us with.

Andy Schlafly, an attorney, is the fifth of Phyllis Schlafly's six children.

About Ed Martin

On September 28, 2015, Phyllis Schlafly named Ed Martin as her hand-picked successor. Ed had been working as a special assistant to Phyllis for more than two years. A lawyer and bioethicist by training, Ed had previously served as chairman of the Missouri Republican Party and chief of staff to Missouri Governor Matt Blunt. Ed works out of the Phyllis Schlafly Center of Washington D.C. and lives in Great Falls, VA, with his wife and four children.